A BOOK OF ARCHÆOLOGY

A BOOK OF ARCHÆOLOGY

SEVENTEEN STORIES OF DISCOVERY

selected and edited by

MARGARET WHEELER

*With 12 pages of half-tone illustrations
and 3 maps*

CASSELL & COMPANY LTD
LONDON

CASSELL & CO LTD

37/38 ST. ANDREW'S HILL, QUEEN VICTORIA STREET

LONDON, E.C.4

and at

210 *Queen Street, Melbourne;* 26/30 *Clarence Street, Sydney;*
24 *Wyndham Street, Auckland, New Zealand;* 1068 *Broadview
Avenue, Toronto* 6; *P.O. Box* 275, *Cape Town; P.O. Box* 11190,
Johannesburg; 58 *Pembroke Street, Port of Spain, Trinidad;
Haroon Chambers, South Napier Road, Karachi;* 13/14 *Ajmeri
Gate Extension, New Delhi* 1; 15 *Graham Road, Ballard Estate,
Bombay* 1; 17 *Chittaranjan Avenue, Calcutta* 13; *Macdonald House,
Orchard Road, Singapore* 9; *P.O. Box* 959, *Accra, Ghana;
Avenida* 9 *de Julho* 1138, *São Paulo; Galeria Güemes, Escritorio*
454/59 *Florida* 165, *Buenos Aires; Marne* 5b, *Mexico* 5, *D.F.;*
25 *rue Henri Barbusse, Paris* 5e; 25 *Ny Strandvej, Espergaerde,
Denmark; Kauwlaan* 17, *The Hague; Bederstrasse* 51, *Zürich* 2.

First published 1957

*Set in 11 point Baskerville type and
made and printed in Great Britain by C. Tinling & Co. Ltd.
Liverpool, London and Prescot.*

F. 657

FOR MY DAUGHTER
ELIZABETH

CONTENTS

ILLUSTRATIONS

LASCAUX: A PAINTED CAVE
17. Frieze of horses with a jumping cow (*Caisse Nationale des Monuments Historiques*)
18. A wounded bison turns on its attacker (*Caisse Nationale des Monuments Historiques*)

THE MYSTERY OF TOLLUND MAN
19. The whole man crouched (*National Museum, Copenhagen*)

THE BOY FROM THE LEAD MOUNTAIN
20. An Inca boy frozen in sleep (*Associated Press*)

POMPEII: A CITY BURIED ALIVE
21. The house of the Vettiorii (*The Mansell Collection*)
22. The Street of Abundance (*The Mansell Collection*)

ILLUSTRATIONS IN THE TEXT

FOREWORD

IMAGINE that it is 2nd June, 1953. You are in a comfortable room and you are riveted to a television set. You see the gingerbread coach of George III bearing Queen Elizabeth II to Westminster Abbey for her Coronation. Soldiers line the route, crowds are cheering, tier upon tier of spectators flicker for an instant upon the screen and then are lost, great buildings appear momentarily—and steadily the horses pace onward towards the ancient Abbey.

How much is here combined to make the day! Much of it will live because we have learnt the art of recording; but what of the peoples who lived before such full written or visual records were kept? They have left only material remains and we can interpret them as best we may, but how dry and shorn of life our picture must necessarily be. In two thousand years— with, we will suppose, all records perished—the ruined found- ations of an Abbey, a gold coach and the lines of tiny post-holes along the route, even a crown and jewels and the quaint boxes that had once been television sets, which lie broken on the crumbled floors of buried houses, will never tell the story of the mid-twentieth century Coronation.

So much, then, we shall never know. What, for instance, were the great ceremonies performed at Stonehenge? Why was the man at Tollund cast into the bog with a halter round his neck? How was the civic organization of early Jericho controlled? These, and a million other problems, must remain a mystery; but what the archæologists have been able to tell us is of tremendous importance.

They have traced the story of man's endeavour to raise himself from a primitive gatherer of wild foods into the complex town-dweller of today. They tell us that, for half a million years or more, man subsisted solely on the food that nature provided, without in any way adding to it by his own efforts; but that during all this long, dark period he was developing and perfecting his tools, and that, eventually, he was able to express himself through art, as shown by cave paintings like those at Lascaux in central France. Then, at last, he learnt to cultivate grain and domesticate animals. He was now able to settle down in one place, and the time came when he built the first town.

What a revolution that was! By having a permanent home he had gained security, and leisure for things higher than the mere struggle for existence. At last he had time to think between meals, and the mind was free to develop ideas and specialize crafts. This was the beginning of civilization.

Archæologists have been able to indicate the lines of man's progress. 'Here,' they say, 'is the earliest town as yet known in the world,' and they point to Jericho, which can be dated by modern scientific methods to about 7,000 B.C. Elsewhere, again, they say 'Here man has learnt the art of making pottery' or 'Here he has learnt to use metal' and 'Here, he has invented writing'. The written records of Mesopotamia and Egypt help archæologists to interpret the story, but the great tomb finds at Ur and Thebes bring us into closer contact with Queen Shub-ad and Tut·ankh·amen than can any sketchy record of those times.

The following extracts are taken from books written by archæologists who either found the remains of bygone peoples, or who have worked upon and studied those findings. Some of the extracts paint a picture of the men of the Old Stone Age, of men who lived when pottery or metal was first known, of kings and queens, art and writing, and although we can read the accounts and marvel, we must remember that it is only a shadow of what must have been.

In compiling these chapters I have received help from many friends and I would like here to record my gratitude to them: Dr. O. G. S. Crawford, C.B.E., who wrote 'Archæology from the Air' specially for this book; Professor M. E. L. Mallowan; Dr. Kathleen Kenyon, C.B.E., with her publisher, Benn Brothers Ltd., who have allowed me to include an extract from her forthcoming book *Jericho: The Oldest Town In The World*; Dr. G. H. S. Bushnell of Cambridge University; Mr. R. L. S. Bruce-Mitford and Mr. A. Digby of the British Museum; Mr. John Hopkins of the library of the Society of Antiquaries; Miss G. Talbot; and Mrs. Ann Orbach who made the translation from the Spanish for 'The Boy from the Lead Mountain'.

MARGARET WHEELER

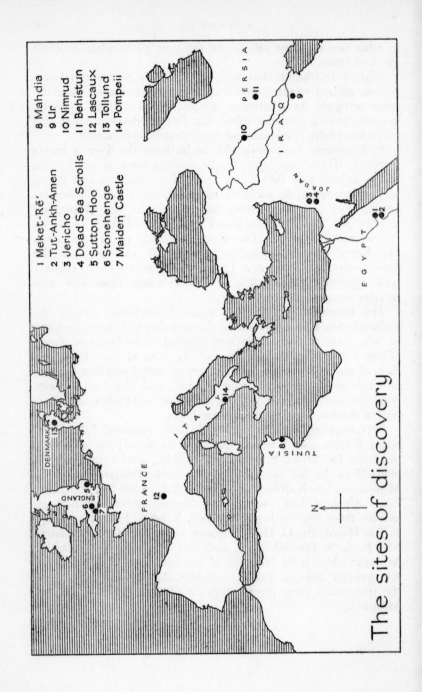

The sites of discovery

1 Meket-Rē'
2 Tut-Ankh-Amen
3 Jericho
4 Dead Sea Scrolls
5 Sutton Hoo
6 Stonehenge
7 Maiden Castle
8 Mahdia
9 Ur
10 Nimrud
11 Behistun
12 Lascaux
13 Tollund
14 Pompeii

EGYPT

H. E. WINLOCK

THE WORLD OF MEKET-RĒ'

(From MODELS OF DAILY LIFE IN ANCIENT EGYPT, FROM THE TOMB OF MEKET-RE'
AT THEBES. *Harvard University Press*, 1955)

To the American, Herbert Winlock, fell the great luck of
discovering the vault of the tomb of an Egyptian nobleman
called Meket-Rē'. Meket-Rē' lived four thousand years ago
and was buried at Thebes on the Upper Nile. His tomb-
chamber was desecrated, but the small vault below the
corridor was never found by the tomb robbers and remained
intact and perfect, with all that it contained, until 17th
March, 1920. Winlock's account describes most vividly all
that he found in that secret room.

I HAD gotten as far on my way home as the ruins of
Medinet Habu. The walls of the old temple were turning
pink in the sunset glow. The water-wheel that drones and
quavers all day under the palms near by was silent for the
night. Way up where the purple shadows were creeping out
of the valleys in the tawny mountain I could see little specks
of men and boys winding down the paths from the work at
the tomb. The evening meal was being prepared and the
bluish smoke of cook fires was beginning to float over Gurnet
Murrai, where the tombs are seething tenements of Arabs and
their flocks. At the house they would be getting tea ready
and I was late.

From the passers-by on the path there broke into my thoughts
a cheerful voice saying: 'May thy night be happy.'

I looked around and recognized one of our workmen,
Abdullahi. 'And may thine be happy and blessed,' I replied,
without checking my donkey, who was far more interested in
getting home to his evening clover than in stopping for wayside
greetings.

But Abdullahi felt otherwise. He must shake hands—quite
an uncalled-for politeness, I thought—and evidently wanted
to stop and chat.

'I am going home,' he informed me, and I said that that
seemed evident. 'And when I get my blankets I am going back
to spend the night at the tomb.' For the life of me I couldn't

remember whether we kept guards up there at night to look after the equipment, but I supposed we must, and as I started on again I laughingly hoped he had something to watch. 'The Headman Hamid says I must tell no one, but Your Honour will see something up there,' Abdullahi called after me.

He had charged his voice with all the mysteriousness he could put into it and his whole manner would have been strange enough to impress me at any other time, but I was convinced of failure, and when I remembered that Abdullahi belonged to one of the gangs which were clearing those corridors out, I knew perfectly well there could be nothing to it at all. Daressy had surely dug those corridors out, and our re-clearing to draw a plan could not possibly show up anything new.

At the house I met Lansing and Hauser coming out. They said they were going up to the work, and showed me a scrap of paper with a hastily scribbled note from Burton: 'Come *at once* and bring your electric torch. Good luck *at last.*' This seemed preposterous. Surely it was another false alarm, and we had had so many of them. However there was Abdullahi and his mysteriousness, and I decided to let my tea wait a while and go with them, but I refused to have any hopes, and the three of us got ready all sorts of sarcasms for Burton's benefit as we trudged along.

A little knot of Arabs was standing around the mouth of the tomb in the twilight. Inside in the gloom we could just make out Burton and the headmen. There was something in the air that made our sarcastic remarks sound flat. Burton pointed to a yawning black crack between the wall of the corridor and the rock floor. He said that he had tried to look in with matches but they didn't give light enough and told us to try the torches.

At least a hole here was unexpected, but we had looked into so many empty holes. Anyway, I got down flat on my stomach, pushed the torch into the hole, pressed the button, and looked in.

The beam of light shot into a little world of four thousand years ago, and I was gazing down into the midst of a myriad of brightly painted little men going this way and that. A tall slender girl gazed across at me perfectly composed; a gang of little men with sticks in their upraised hands drove spotted oxen; rowers tugged at their oars on a fleet of boats, while one ship seemed foundering right in front of me with its bow balanced precariously in the air. And all of this busy going and coming was in uncanny silence, as though the distance back over the forty centuries I looked across was too great for even an echo to reach my ears.

I was completely stupefied when I gave my torch to the others and one by one they looked in through the crack. It was almost night now and we saw that we could do nothing until the morning. While the other two went back to the house to get some sealing-wax and cord, Burton and I sat down dazedly to talk it over. He told me how he had been coming down from the mountain-top where he had been taking photographs and had stopped at the work to dismiss the men as usual. As he expected, they had cleared most of the fallen stone from the corridors, but just before he had come along one of the men in this one had noticed that the chips had an unaccountable way of trickling into a crack as fast as he dug. At first the man hadn't paid much attention. It was just one of those crazy whims of the Americans that had made them want to dig out such a place anyway. Still, he had called the headman of his gang and together they were scraping away the stones from the crack when Burton had arrived.

When we left the tomb for the night the crack was stopped up with stones and stretched across with strings securely sealed with sealing-wax—quite a little of which was on my fingers. The gang which was working in the corridor had received all sorts of needless instructions about keeping someone on watch all night. None of them slept a wink for the next three nights, I am sure, sitting in the starlight in front of the tomb discussing the baksheesh they hoped to get. We were no less excited. That night we sat up late discussing what the place could be, each one of us dwelling at length on some marvel he alone had seen. I believe someone claimed to have seen Santa Claus and his eight tiny reindeer—or possibly I dreamed I had seen him. Anyway, I for one woke up in the morning with a raging headache that was made no better by trying to seem masterfully calm.

In the morning our work began, and three terrific days followed. Burton rigged up mirrors to throw sunlight down the corridor and took a photograph of the crack in the rocks. Then we dug in front of it and found in the floor of the corridor a little pit, about a yard square and waist-deep. It had been carefully filled with chips of the very rock it was cut in, and both ancient thieves and modern archæologists had taken this filling for the living rock of the mountain and passed over it. The side of the pit under the wall of the corridor was built up of mud bricks, and when we had photographed them and taken them away we were looking down into a little low chamber about three yards square and scarcely four feet high, into which no man had entered for four thousand years. Rock had fallen from the roof—in doing so it had opened up the crack we had looked into the night before—and had up-ended one of the boats and broken others, but except for this nothing had been disturbed. Our only fear was that as fresh air got into the chamber more would come tumbling down, and we were torn between a desire to get everything out safely before we had a catastrophe and to get a complete set of photographs and plans of everything just as we had found it. It was just luck that made both possible, for after we were finished tons of rock began to fall in the tomb. Still we escaped the misfortunes of our French colleagues digging half a mile away. They had a man killed by rock falling in a tomb chamber while we were working in this one.

We photographed, we planned, we carefully cleared away chips of fallen stone, and then we lifted out one or two of the boats or a group of little men and began all over again. One night will always remain a weird picture in my mind. Lansing and I had gone up to clear away more of the fallen shale to get ready for Burton's photographs in the morning. From afar off we began to halloo to the guards, for we had lent them a couple of revolvers and we were afraid of the zeal they might show in their use of them in the dark. Duly challenged, we made our way up the slope and inside the tomb, and lit candles to work by. For hours we worked away, the shadowy Arabs pattering barefooted back and forth from the flickering candle-light out into the open, where the brilliant desert stars seemed to hang right down to the mouth of the gloomy tunnel.

As we worked along through those three days and nights we began to realize what it was that we had so unexpectedly discovered. The tomb was that of a great noble of four thousand years ago. He himself had been buried in a gilded coffin and a sarcophagus of stone in a mortuary chamber deep down under the back of the corridor, where the thieves had destroyed everything ages before our day. Only this little chamber had escaped and it was turning out to be a sort of secret closet where the provisions were stored for the future life of the great man.

He could not conceive of an existence in which he would not require food and drink, clothing and housing, such as he was used to in this life, and being a rich man, naturally he wanted an estate in eternity like that which he had owned on earth. His philosophy carried him beyond that of the savage chieftain who expects a horde of servants to be slaughtered at his grave. He attained the same end by putting in his tomb a host of little wooden servants, carved and painted, at their daily tasks, working before little portraits of himself. The spirits of these little servants worked eternally, turning out spirit food or sailing ships upon a spirit Nile, and his soul could enter any one of the little portraits of himself at will to reap the harvest of their labours. In short we had found a picture of the life the great noble hoped to live in eternity, which was nothing more or less than the one he had led on earth forty centuries ago.

The first thing we had seen when we had peeped through the crack had been a big model nearly six feet long, showing a noble seated on a porch among his scribes, taking the count of his cattle as they were driven past [Fig. 1]. In the back of the room we found, under a lot of other models, neatly stacked, the stable where these same cattle were being fattened, and finally when we came to move one big boxlike affair in the far corner —a model I had tried my best to get a peep into and almost fallen headlong in the process—we found it was the butcher shop where the cattle's life history ended [Fig. 2]. The night we worked in the tomb by lamplight we got a peep into a granary where diminutive scribes sat writing down the quantity of grain being measured and carried to the bins by hard-working labourers. And later we ran across the bakery where the grain was ground and made into loaves and the brewery where the home beverage was being fermented in tall crocks and then decanted into round-bellied jugs. Lansing extracted two canoes manned by fishermen who hauled a miraculous draught of painted catfish and perch in a seine, and I picked the fallen stones out of two gardens in which copper ponds—that would hold real water—were surrounded by little wooden fig-trees and cool, shady porches. Then there was a carpenter shop and another shop where women spun thread and wove cloth. The very threads on their distaffs and spindles—frail as cobwebs though they were with age—had remained unbroken in that eternal stillness.

The business of the great man entailed a lot of travelling, and his idle hours were passed in pleasure sails or fishing trips on the Nile or on the still backwaters of the marshes. On the celestial Nile he would want to go voyaging or yachting, too, and therefore a dozen model boats were put in the chamber. We found them setting sail, the captain bossing the sailors who sway on the halyards and set the backstays. A man throws his whole weight against the pole as they put off from the bank and another stands by in the bow with a fender in case they bump against another vessel. When they travel down-stream against the north wind the mast and sail are lowered and the crew man the sweeps. The noble himself sits under the awning in front of the cabin smelling a lotus flower while his son sits on deck beside him and they both listen to a singer and an old blind harper. Inside the cabin squats a steward beside the bunk, under which are shoved two little round-topped leather trunks. A kitchen-boat follows, and the cooks get ready a meal to be served when evening comes and they are moored to the bank. There were yachts, to be sailed with the wind or paddled against it, and a low raking skiff, from the bow of which two men are casting harpoons while others land an enormous fish over the side.

Thus had the great man lived and so did he expect to live after he had gone to his 'eternal abode', as he called it. Finally, the funeral day had come. His body was brought across the river from Thebes, through the green fields, where the wondering peasants leaned on their hoes to watch it pass, and then up through the rocky gorges to his tomb. A long procession followed him, each model borne on the head of one of his serfs, and a crowd of peasant girls and women from his estates brought baskets of wine and beer and baked meats for the funeral banquet. Even their contributions were expected to go on for ever, and statues of two of them, half life-sized, had been made to go with the models in the chamber. There we found them towering above the horde of miniature men and beasts, looking over at us with grave, wide-open eyes. Four thousand years they had stood thus silent—if only we could have broken that silence and got from them the secret of the pattern their tightly clinging dresses were made on, we were sure we could

have made a killing in the suit and clothing trade in the New
York of today.

Four thousand years is an eternity. Just saying it over and
over again gives no conception of the ages that have gone by
since that funeral. Stop and think of how far off William the
Conqueror seems. That takes you only a quarter of the way
back. Julius Cæsar takes you half-way back. With Saul and
David you are three-fourths of the way, but there remains
another thousand years to bridge with your imagination. Yet
in that dry, still, dark little chamber those boats and statues
had stood indifferent to all that went on in the outer world,
as ancient in the days of Cæsar as Cæsar is to us, but so little
changed that even the finger-prints of the men who put them
there were still fresh upon them. Not only finger-prints but
even fly-specks, cobwebs, and dead spiders remained from the
time when these models were stored in some empty room
waiting for the day of death and burial. I even suspect that
some of his grandchildren had sneaked in and played with
them while they were at that house in ancient Thebes, for
some of them were broken in a way that is hard to explain
otherwise. Possibly that is a wild guess, but at any rate there
is no doubt of what had happened to them in the little chamber
in the tomb on the day of the funeral. After all of the models
had been stowed away and the masons had come to brick up
the doorway, they had found one of the boats in their way.
So one of them picked it up and laid it to one side on top of
the granary, and under bow and stern he left a great smear of
the mud he had just been mixing for mortar. There those
smears still remain.

The little models had to be parted after all these ages
together. Half of them went to the Egyptian Government,
under the terms of our concession, and are now on view in
the museum in Cairo. The others can be seen in the Metropolitan Museum in New York. If any reader should see them
there in their glass cases he will get a far better first view of
them than we did with our electric torches flashing through
that crack in the rock—but none of us would swap places with
him. They meant too much to us that evening when we were
wondering where we would dig next.

HOWARD CARTER AND A. C. MACE

TUT·ANKH·AMEN: THE WEALTH OF AN EGYPTIAN KING

(FROM THE TOMB OF TUT·ANKH·AMEN. *Cassell*, 1927)

'We made a discovery that far exceeded our wildest dreams.' In the following extract Mr. Howard Carter tells how he found the tomb of Tut·ankh·amen, the young Pharaoh who ruled Egypt for a few years from 1357 B.C. The ancient Egyptians believed that they must take with them into the next world, not only their preserved bodies, but all the worldly paraphernalia to make that life enjoyable. There had been the period of the mighty pyramid tombs, but the riches buried in them were so great that they were often plundered within a few years of their completion. Later the Kings were interred in the more discreet Valley of the Kings on the Upper Nile, and it was here, in 1922, that Mr. Howard Carter and the Earl of Carnarvon made the most spectacular discovery of modern times. The Tut·ankh·amen treasure can now be seen in the Cairo Museum.

THIS was to be our final season in The Valley. Six full seasons we had excavated there, and season after season had drawn a blank; we had worked for months at a stretch and found nothing, and only an excavator knows how desperately depressing that can be; we had almost made up our minds that we were beaten, and were preparing to leave The Valley and try our luck elsewhere; and then—hardly had we set hoe to ground in our last despairing effort than we made a discovery that far exceeded our wildest dreams. Surely, never before in the whole history of excavation has a full digging season been compressed within the space of five days.

Let me try and tell the story of it all. It will not be easy, for the dramatic suddenness of the initial discovery left me in a dazed condition, and the months that have followed have been so crowded with incident that I have hardly had time to think. Setting it down on paper will perhaps give me a chance to realize what has happened and all that it means.

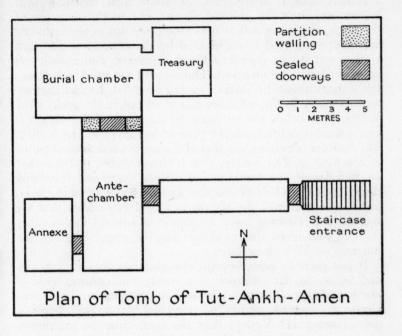

Partition walling

Sealed doorways

0 1 2 3 4 5
METRES

Treasury

Burial chamber

Ante-chamber

Annexe

N

Staircase entrance

Plan of Tomb of Tut-Ankh-Amen

I arrived in Luxor on 28th October, and by 1st November I had enrolled my workmen and was ready to begin. Our former excavations had stopped short at the north-east corner of the tomb of Rameses VI, and from this point I started trenching southwards. It will be remembered that in this area there were a number of roughly constructed workmen's huts, used probably by the labourers in the tomb of Rameses. These huts, built about three feet above bed-rock, covered the whole area in front of the Ramesside tomb, and continued in a southerly direction to join up with a similar group of huts on the opposite side of The Valley, discovered by Davis in connexion with his work on the Akh·en·Aten cache. By the evening of 3rd November we had laid bare a sufficient number of these huts for experimental purposes, so, after we had planned and noted them, they were removed, and we were ready to clear away the three feet of soil that lay beneath them.

Hardly had I arrived on the work next morning (4th November) than the unusual silence, due to the stoppage of the work, made me realize that something out of the ordinary had happened, and I was greeted by the announcement that a steep cut in the rock had been discovered underneath the very first hut to be attacked. This seemed too good to be true, but a short amount of extra clearing revealed the fact that we were actually in the entrance of a steep cut in the rock, some thirteen feet below the entrance to the tomb of Rameses VI, and a similar depth from the present bed level of The Valley. The manner of cutting was that of the sunken stairway entrance so common in The Valley, and I almost dared to hope that we had found our tomb at last. Work continued feverishly throughout the whole of that day and the morning of the next, but it was not until the afternoon of 5th November that we succeeded in clearing away the masses of rubbish that overlay the cut, and were able to demarcate the upper edges of the stairway on all its four sides.

It was clear by now, beyond any question, that we actually had before us the entrance to a tomb, but doubts, born of previous disappointments, persisted in creeping in. There was always the horrible possibility, suggested by our experience in the Thotmes III Valley, that the tomb was an unfinished one, never completed and never used; if it had been finished there was the depressing probability that it had been completely plundered in ancient times. On the other hand, there was just the chance of an untouched or only partially plundered tomb, and it was with ill-suppressed excitement that I watched the descending steps of the staircase, as one by one they came to light. The cutting was excavated in the side of a small hillock, and, as the work progressed, its western edge receded under the slope of the rock until it was, first partially, and then completely, roofed in, and became a passage, ten feet high by six feet wide. Work progressed more rapidly now; step succeeded step, and at the level of the twelfth, towards sunset, there was disclosed the upper part of a doorway, blocked, plastered, and sealed.

A sealed doorway—it was actually true, then! Our years of patient labour were to be rewarded after all, and I think my first feeling was one of congratulation that my faith in The Valley had not been unjustified. With excitement growing to fever-heat I searched the seal impressions on the door for evidence of the identity of the owner, but could find no name: the only decipherable ones were those of the well-known royal necropolis seal, the jackal and nine captives. Two facts, however, were clear: first, the employment of this royal seal was certain evidence that the tomb had been constructed for a person of very high standing; and second, that the sealed door was entirely screened from above by workmen's huts of the Twentieth Dynasty was sufficiently clear proof that at least from that date it had never been entered. With that for the moment I had to be content.

While examining the seals I noticed, at the top of the doorway, where some of the plaster had fallen away, a heavy wooden lintel. Under this, to assure myself of the method by which the doorway had been blocked, I made a small peephole, just large enough to insert an electric torch, and discovered that the passage beyond the door was filled completely from floor to ceiling with stones and rubble—additional proof, this, of the care with which the tomb had been protected.

It was a thrilling moment for an excavator. Alone, save for my native workmen, I found myself, after years of comparatively unproductive labour, on the threshold of what might prove to be a magnificent discovery. Anything, literally anything, might lie beyond that passage, and it needed all my self-control to keep from breaking down the doorway, and investigating then and there.

One thing puzzled me, and that was the smallness of the opening in comparison with the ordinary Valley tombs. The design was certainly of the Eighteenth Dynasty. Could it be the tomb of a noble buried here by royal consent? Was it a royal cache, a hiding-place to which a mummy and its equipment had been removed for safety? Or was it actually the tomb of the king for whom I had spent so many years in search?

Once more I examined the seal impression for a clue, but on the part of the door so far laid bare only those of the royal necropolis seal already mentioned were clear enough to read. Had I but known that a few inches lower down there was a perfectly clear and distinct impression of the seal of Tut·ankh· Amen, the King I most desired to find, I would have cleared on, had a much better night's rest in consequence, and saved myself nearly three weeks of uncertainty. It was late, however, and darkness was already upon us. With some reluctance I reclosed the small hole that I had made, filled in our excavation for protection during the night, selected the most trustworthy of my workmen—themselves almost as excited as I was—to watch all night above the tomb, and so home by moonlight, riding down The Valley.

Naturally my wish was to go straight ahead with our clearing to find the full extent of the discovery, but Lord Carnarvon was in England, and in fairness to him I had to delay matters until he could come. Accordingly, on the morning of 6th November, I sent him the following cable: 'At last have made wonderful discovery in Valley; a magnificent tomb with seals intact; re-covered same for your arrival; congratulations.'

My next task was to secure the doorway against interference until such time as it could finally be reopened. This we did by filling our excavation up again to surface level, and rolling on top of it the large flint boulders of which the workmen's huts had been composed. By the evening of the same day, exactly forty-eight hours after we had discovered the first step of the staircase, this was accomplished. The tomb had vanished. So far as the appearance of the ground was concerned there never had been any tomb, and I found it hard to persuade myself at times that the whole episode had not been a dream.

I was soon to be reassured on this point. News travels fast in Egypt, and within two days of the discovery congratulations, inquiries, and offers of help descended upon me in a steady stream from all directions. It became clear, even at this early stage, that I was in for a job that could not be tackled single-handed, so I wired to Callender, who had helped me on various previous occasions, asking him if possible to join me without delay, and to my relief he arrived on the very next day. On the 8th I had received two messages from Lord Carnarvon in answer to my cable, the first of which read: 'Possibly come soon,' and the second, received a little later: 'Propose arrive Alexandria 20th.'

We had thus nearly a fortnight's grace, and we devoted it to making preparations of various kinds, so that when the time of reopening came, we should be able, with the least possible delay, to handle any situation that might arise. On the night of the 18th I went to Cairo for three days, to meet Lord Carnarvon and make a number of necessary purchases, returning to Luxor on the 21st. On the 23rd Lord Carnarvon arrived in Luxor with his daughter, Lady Evelyn Herbert, his devoted companion in all his Egyptian work, and everything was in hand for the beginning of the second chapter of the discovery of the tomb. Callender had been busy all day clearing away the upper layer of rubbish, so that by morning we should be able to get into the staircase without any delay.

By the afternoon of the 24th the whole staircase was clear, sixteen steps in all, and we were able to make a proper examination of the sealed doorway. On the lower part the seal impressions were much clearer, and we were able without any difficulty to make out on several of them the name of Tut·ankh·Amen. This added enormously to the interest of the discovery. If we had found, as seemed almost certain, the tomb of that shadowy monarch, whose tenure of the throne coincided with one of the most interesting periods in the whole of Egyptian history, we should indeed have reason to congratulate ourselves.

With heightened interest, if that were possible, we renewed our investigation of the doorway. Here for the first time a disquieting element made its appearance. Now that the whole door was exposed to light it was possible to discern a fact that had hitherto escaped notice—that there had been two successive openings and reclosings of a part of its surface: furthermore, that the sealing originally discovered, the jackal and nine captives, had been applied to the reclosed portions, whereas the sealings of Tut·ankh·Amen covered the untouched part of the doorway, and were therefore those with which the tomb had been originally secured. The tomb then was not absolutely intact, as we had hoped. Plunderers had entered it, and entered it more than once—from the evidence of the huts above, plunderers of a date not later than the reign of Rameses VI—but that they had not rifled it completely was evident from the fact that it had been re-sealed.

Then came another puzzle. In the lower strata of rubbish that filled the staircase we found masses of broken potsherds and boxes, the latter bearing the names of Akh·en·Aten, Smenkh·ka·Re and Tut·ankh·Amen, and, what was much more upsetting, a scarab of Thotmes III and a fragment with the name of Amen·hetep III. Why this mixture of names? The balance of evidence so far would seem to indicate a cache rather than a tomb, and at this stage in the proceedings we inclined more and more to the opinion that we were about to find a miscellaneous collection of objects of the Eighteenth

Dynasty kings, brought from Tell el Amarna by Tut·ankh·
Amen and deposited here for safety.

So matters stood on the evening of the 24th. On the following day the sealed doorway was to be removed, so Callender
set carpenters to work making a heavy wooden grille to be
set up in its place. Mr. Engelbach, Chief Inspector of the
Antiquities Department, paid us a visit during the afternoon,
and witnessed part of the final clearing of rubbish from the
doorway.

On the morning of the 25th the seal impressions on the
doorway were carefully noted and photographed, and then we
removed the actual blocking of the door, consisting of rough
stones carefully built from floor to lintel, and heavily plastered
on their outer faces to take the seal impressions.

This disclosed the beginning of a descending passage (not a
staircase), the same width as the entrance stairway, and nearly
seven feet high. As I had already discovered from my hole in
the doorway, it was filled completely with stone and rubble,
probably the chip from its own excavation. This filling, like
the doorway, showed distinct signs of more than one opening
and reclosing of the tomb, the untouched part consisting of
clean white chip, mingled with dust, whereas the disturbed
part was composed mainly of dark flint. It was clear that an
irregular tunnel had been cut through the original filling at
the upper corner on the left side, a tunnel corresponding in
position with that of the hole in the doorway.

As we cleared the passage we found, mixed with the rubble
of the lower levels, broken potsherds, jar sealings, alabaster
jars, whole and broken, vases of painted pottery, numerous
fragments of smaller articles, and water-skins, these last having
obviously been used to bring up the water needed for the
plastering of the doorways. These were clear evidence of
plundering, and we eyed them askance. By night we had
cleared a considerable distance down the passage, but as yet
saw no sign of a second doorway or of a chamber.

The day following (26th November) was the day of days,
the most wonderful that I have ever lived through, and
certainly one whose like I can never hope to see again.
Throughout the morning the work of clearing continued,
slowly perforce, on account of the delicate objects that were
mixed with the filling. Then, in the middle of the afternoon,
thirty feet down from the outer door, we came upon a second

sealed doorway, almost an exact replica of the first. The seal impressions in this case were less distinct, but still recognizable as those of Tut·ankh·Amen and of the royal necropolis. Here again the signs of opening and reclosing were clearly marked upon the plaster. We were firmly convinced by this time that it was a cache that we were about to open, and not a tomb. The arrangement of stairway, entrance passage, and doors reminded us very forcibly of the cache of Akh·en·Aten and Tyi material found in the very near vicinity of the present excavation by Davis, and the fact that Tut·ankh·Amen's seals occurred there likewise seemed almost certain proof that we were right in our conjecture. We were soon to know. There lay the sealed doorway, and behind it was the answer to the question.

Slowly, desperately slowly it seemed to us as we watched, the remains of passage debris that encumbered the lower part of the doorway were removed, until at last we had the whole door clear before us. The decisive moment had arrived. With trembling hands I made a tiny breach in the upper left-hand corner. Darkness and blank space, as far as an iron testing-rod could reach, showed that whatever lay beyond was empty and not filled like the passage we had just cleared. Candle tests were applied as a precaution against possible foul gases, and then, widening the hole a little, I inserted the candle and peered in, Lord Carnarvon, Lady Evelyn, and Callender standing anxiously beside me to hear the verdict. At first I could see nothing, the hot air escaping from the chamber causing the candle flame to flicker, but presently, as my eyes grew accustomed to the light, details of the room within emerged slowly from the mist, strange animals, statues, and gold—everywhere the glint of gold. For the moment—an eternity it must have seemed to the others standing by—I was struck dumb with amazement, and when Lord Carnarvon, unable to stand the suspense any longer, inquired anxiously, 'Can you see anything?' it was all I could do to get out the words, 'Yes, wonderful things.' Then widening the hole a little further, so that we both could see, we inserted an electric torch.

I suppose most excavators would confess to a feeling of awe —embarrassment almost—when they break into a chamber closed and sealed by pious hands so many centuries ago. For the moment, time as a factor in human life has lost its meaning.

Three thousand, four thousand years maybe, have passed and gone since human feet last trod the floor on which you stand, and yet, as you note the signs of recent life around you—the half-filled bowl of mortar for the door, the blackened lamp, the finger-mark upon the freshly painted surface, the farewell garland dropped upon the threshold—you feel it might have been but yesterday. The very air you breathe, unchanged throughout the centuries, you share with those who laid the mummy to its rest. Time is annihilated by little intimate details such as these, and you feel an intruder.

That is perhaps the first and dominant sensation, but others follow thick and fast—the exhilaration of discovery, the fever of suspense, the almost overmastering impulse, born of curiosity, to break down seals and lift the lids of boxes, the thought—pure joy to the investigator—that you are about to add a page to history, or solve some problem of research, the strained expectancy—why not confess it?—of the treasure-seeker. Did these thoughts actually pass through our minds at the time, or have I imagined them since? I cannot tell. It was the discovery that my memory was blank, and not the mere desire for dramatic chapter-ending, that occasioned this digression.

Surely never before in the whole history of excavation had such an amazing sight been seen as the light of our torch revealed to us. The reader can get some idea of it by reference to the photograph [Fig. 4], but this was taken afterwards when the tomb had been opened and electric light installed. Let him imagine how they appeared to us as we looked down upon them from our spy-hole in the blocked doorway, casting the beam of light from our torch—the first light that had pierced the darkness of the chamber for three thousand years—from one group of objects to another, in a vain attempt to interpret the treasure that lay before us. The effect was bewildering, overwhelming. I suppose we had never formulated exactly in our minds just what we had expected or hoped to see, but certainly we had never dreamed of anything like this, a roomful—a whole museumful it seemed—of objects, some familiar, but some the like of which we had never seen, piled one upon another in seemingly endless profusion.

Gradually the scene grew clearer, and we could pick out individual objects. First, right opposite to us—we had been conscious of them all the while, but refused to believe in them

—were three great gilt couches, their sides carved in the form
of monstrous animals, curiously attenuated in body, as they
had to be to serve their purpose, but with heads of startling
realism. Uncanny beasts enough to look upon at any time:
seen as we saw them, their brilliant gilded surfaces picked out
of the darkness by our electric torch, as though by limelight,
their heads throwing grotesque distorted shadows on the wall
behind them, they were almost terrifying. Next, on the right,
two statues caught and held our attention; two life-sized
figures of a king in black, facing each other like sentinels, gold
kilted, gold sandalled, armed with mace and staff, the protective sacred cobra upon their foreheads.

These were the dominant objects that caught the eye at
first. Between them, around them, piled on top of them, there
were countless others—exquisitely painted and inlaid caskets;
alabaster vases, some beautifully carved in open-work designs;
strange black shrines, from the open door of one a great gilt
snake peeping out; bouquets of flowers or leaves; beds; chairs
beautifully carved; a golden inlaid throne; a heap of curious
white oviform boxes; staves of all shapes and designs; beneath
our eyes, on the very threshold of the chamber, a beautiful
lotiform cup of translucent alabaster; on the left a confused
pile of overturned chariots, glistening with gold and inlay;
and peeping from behind them another portrait of the king.

Such were some of the objects that lay before us. Whether
we noted them all at the time I cannot say for certain, as our
minds were in much too excited and confused a state to register
accurately. Presently it dawned upon our bewildered brains
that in all this medley of objects before us there was no coffin
or trace of a mummy, and the much-debated question of tomb
or cache began to intrigue us afresh. With this question in
view we re-examined the scene before us, and noticed for the
first time that between the two black sentinel statues on the
right there was another sealed doorway. The explanation
gradually dawned upon us. We were but on the threshold of
our discovery. What we saw was merely an antechamber.
Behind the guarded door there were to be other chambers,
possibly a succession of them, and in one of them, beyond any
shadow of doubt, in all his magnificent panoply of death, we
should find the Pharaoh lying.

We had seen enough, and our brains began to reel at the
thought of the task in front of us. We reclosed the hole, locked

the wooden grille that had been placed upon the first doorway, left our native staff on guard, mounted our donkeys and rode home down The Valley, strangely silent and subdued.

It was curious, as we talked things over in the evening, to find how conflicting our ideas were as to what we had seen. Each of us had noted something that the others had not, and it amazed us next day to discover how many and how obvious were the things that we had missed. Naturally, it was the sealed door between the statues that intrigued us most, and we debated far into the night the possibilities of what might lie behind it. A single chamber with the king's sarcophagus? That was the least we might expect. But why one chamber only? Why not a succession of passages and chambers, leading, in true Valley style, to an innermost shrine of all, the burial chamber? It might be so, and yet in plan the tomb was quite unlike the others. Visions of chamber after chamber, each crowded with objects like the one we had seen, passed through our minds and left us gasping for breath. Then came the thought of the plunderers again. Had they succeeded in penetrating this third doorway—seen from a distance it looked absolutely untouched—and, if so, what were our chances of finding the king's mummy intact? I think we slept but little, all of us, that night.

Next morning (27th November) we were early on the field, for there was much to be done. It was essential, before proceeding further with our examination, that we should have some more adequate means of illumination, so Callender began laying wires to connect us up with the main lighting system of The Valley. While this was in preparation we made careful notes of the seal-impressions upon the inner doorway and then removed its entire blocking. By noon everything was ready and Lord Carnarvon, Lady Evelyn, Callender and I entered the tomb and made a careful inspection of the first chamber (afterwards called the Antechamber). The evening before, I had written to Mr. Engelbach, the Chief Inspector of the Antiquities Department, advising him of the progress of clearing, and asking him to come over and make an official inspection. Unfortunately he was at the moment in Kena on official business, so the local Antiquities Inspector, Ibrahim Effendi, came in his stead.

By the aid of our powerful electric lamps many things that had been obscure to us on the previous day became clear, and we were able to make a more accurate estimate of the extent of our discovery. Our first objective was naturally the sealed door between the statues, and here a disappointment awaited us. Seen from a distance it presented all the appearance of an absolutely intact blocking, but close examination revealed the fact that a small breach had been made near the bottom, just wide enough to admit a boy or a slightly built man, and that the hole made had subsequently been filled up and re-sealed. We were not then to be the first. Here, too, the thieves had forestalled us, and it only remained to be seen how much damage they had had the opportunity or the time to effect.

Our natural impulse was to break down the door, and get to the bottom of the matter at once, but to do so would have entailed serious risk of damage to many of the objects in the Antechamber, a risk which we were by no means prepared to face. Nor could we move the objects in question out of the way, for it was imperative that a plan and complete photographic record should be made before anything was touched, and this was a task involving a considerable amount of time, even if we had had sufficient plant available—which we had not—to carry it through immediately. Reluctantly we decided to abandon the opening of this inner sealed door until we had cleared the Antechamber of all its contents. By doing this we should not only ensure the complete scientific record of the outer chamber which it was our duty to make, but should have a clear field for the removal of the door-blocking, a ticklish operation at best.

(*They clear the Antechamber.*)

When we entered the Burial Chamber we found, lying beside a small hole made by the robbers through the masonry of the door, which had been subsequently reclosed by the ancient Egyptian officials, portions of two necklaces dropped by a thief. Around the four sides of the great shrine, which occupied almost the entire area of the chamber, were divers objects and emblems. . . .

At the eastern end of the shrine were two massive folding doors closed with ebony bolts shot into copper staples, their panels decorated with strange figures—headless demon guardians of the caverns of the Underworld. Before these doors stood an exquisite triple-lamp of floral form, carved out of a single block of translucent calcite, in shape three lotiform cups, with stems and leaves springing from a single circular base. . . .

In front, standing along the east wall, was Amen's sacred goose of wood, varnished black, and swathed in linen; beside it were two rush-work baskets collapsed with age, and a wine-jar bearing the legend: 'Year 5, wine of the house of (?) Tut·ankh·Amen, from the Western river Chief of the Vintners, Kha.'

Resting upon the ground, between the shrine and the north wall, were magic oars to ferry the king's barque across the waters of the Nether World. . . .

When we drew back those ebony bolts of the great shrine, the doors swung back as if only closed yesterday, and revealed within yet another shrine, in type like the first, save for the blue inlay. It had similarly bolted doors, but upon them was a seal intact, bearing the name of Tut·ankh·Amen and a recumbent jackal over Egypt's nine foes. Above the shrine drooped a linen pall. This bespangled linen pall, brown with age, still hanging on its curious wooden supports, was rent by the weight of the gilt bronze marguerites sewn to its fabric. The shrine, dazzling from the brilliance of its gold, was decorated with scenes wrought, in beautiful incised-relief, from the book *Of that which is in the Underworld*—that guide to the Hereafter, which points out to the deceased the road he should take, and explains to him the various malefic powers he must meet during his subterranean journey. According to this book two routes led him to the Land of the Blessed, one by water, the other by land, and it further shows that there were byways leading to seething rivers of fire by which he must not travel.

The pall made us realize that we were in the presence of a dead king of past ages. The unbroken seal upon the closed doors of the second shrine gave us the data we were seeking. Had the tomb robbers, who had entered the Antechamber, its Annexe, the Burial Chamber and its Store-room, by any chance reached the king? The shrine was intact, its doors bore their original seal uninjured, indicating that the robbers had not reached him. Henceforth, we knew that, within the shrine, we should be treading where no one had entered, and that we should be dealing with material untouched and unharmed since the boy king was laid to rest nearly three thousand three hundred years ago. . . .

On either side, between the two shrines, stacked in the right and left corners, were numerous ceremonial maces, sticks, staves and bows, some carefully wrapped in linen. Perhaps the choicest of them all were the gold and silver sticks, made of two thin tubular shafts supporting tiny statuettes of the youthful monarch, cast and chased in their respective metals. . . .

The doors of this second shrine were bolted top and bottom, and carefully fastened with cord tied to metal staples and sealed. The clay seal upon this cord was intact. It bore impressions of two distinct seals, one bearing Tut·ankh·Amen's prenomen, Kheperu·neb·Re, surmounting 'A Jackal over nine Foes', the second bore the device of the Royal Necropolis Seal, 'The Jackal over nine Foes', without other distinguishing mark or royal insignia. Here was a great piece of luck, as manifestly behind those two seals we should be dealing with material unharmed since the burial of the king. It was with great care that the cords were severed, and those folding doors opened which, when swung back, revealed yet a third shrine, also sealed and intact—the seal-impressions upon this third shrine being identical to those on the second.

At this point of our undertaking we realized that it would now be possible, by opening those further doors, to solve the secret the shrines had so jealously guarded throughout the centuries. I therefore decided before any other procedure to make the experiment. It was an exciting moment in our arduous task that cannot easily be forgotten. We were to witness a spectacle such as no other man in our times had been privileged to see. With suppressed excitement I carefully cut the cord, removed that precious seal, drew back the bolts, and opened the doors, when a fourth shrine was revealed, similar in design and even more brilliant in workmanship than the last. The decisive moment was at hand! An indescribable moment for an archæologist! What was beneath and what did that fourth shrine contain? With intense excitement I drew back the bolts of the last and unsealed doors; they slowly swung open, and there, filling the entire area within, effectually barring any further progress, stood an immense yellow quartzite sarcophagus, intact, with the lid still firmly fixed in its place, just as the pious hands had left it. It was certainly a thrilling moment, as we gazed upon the spectacle enhanced by the striking contrast—the glitter of metal—of the golden shrines shielding it. Especially striking were the outstretched hand and wing of a goddess sculptured on the end of the sarcophagus, as if to ward off an intruder. It symbolized an idea beautiful in conception and, indeed, seemed an eloquent illustration of the perfect faith and tender solicitude for the well-being of their loved one, that animated the people who dwelt in that land over thirty centuries ago.

We were now able to profit by the experience we had acquired and had a much clearer conception of the operation immediately before us: the three remaining shrines would have to be taken to pieces and removed before the problem of the sarcophagus could be contemplated.

The tackle for raising the lid of the sarcophagus was in position. I gave the word. Amid intense silence the huge slab, broken in two, weighing over a ton and a quarter, rose from its bed. The light shone into the sarcophagus. A sight met our eyes that at first puzzled us. It was a little disappointing. The contents were completely covered by fine linen shrouds. The lid being suspended in mid-air, we rolled back those covering shrouds, one by one, and as the last was removed a gasp of wonderment escaped our lips, so gorgeous was the sight that met our eyes: a golden effigy of the young boy king, of most magnificent workmanship, filled the whole of the interior of the sarcophagus. [Fig. 3]. This was the lid of a wonderful anthropoid coffin, some seven feet in length, resting upon a low bier in the form of a lion, and no doubt the outermost coffin of a series of coffins, nested one within the other, enclosing the mortal remains of the king. Enclasping the body of this magnificent monument were two winged goddesses, Isis and Neith, wrought in rich gold-work upon gesso, as brilliant as the day the coffin was made. To it an additional charm was added, by the fact that, while this decoration was rendered in fine low bas-relief, the head and hands of the king were in the round, in massive gold of the finest sculpture, surpassing anything we could have imagined. The hands, crossed over the breast, held the royal emblems—the Crook and the Flail—encrusted with deep blue faience. The face and features were wonderfully wrought in sheet-gold. The eyes were of aragonite and obsidian, the eyebrows and eyelids inlaid with lapis lazuli glass. There was a touch of realism, for while the rest of this anthropoid coffin, covered with feathered ornament, was of brilliant gold, that of the bare face and hands seemed different, the gold of the flesh being of different alloy, thus conveying an impression of the greyness of death. Upon the forehead of this recumbent figure of the young boy king were two emblems delicately worked in brilliant inlay—the Cobra and the Vulture—symbols of Upper and Lower Egypt, but perhaps the most touching by its human simplicity was the tiny wreath of flowers around these symbols, as it pleased us to think, the last farewell offering of the widowed girl queen to her husband, the youthful representative of the 'Two Kingdoms'.

Among all that regal splendour, that royal magnificence—everywhere the glint of gold—there was nothing so beautiful as those few withered flowers, still retaining their tinge of colour. They told us what a short period three thousand three hundred years really is—but Yesterday and the Morrow. In fact, that little touch of nature made that ancient and our modern civilization kin.

Thus from stairway, steep descending passage, Antechamber and Burial Chamber, from those golden shrines and from that noble sarcophagus, our eyes were now turned to its contents—a gold encased coffin, in form a recumbent figure of the young king, symbolizing Osiris or, it would seem, by its fearless gaze, man's ancient trust in immortality. Many and disturbing were our emotions awakened by that Osiride form. Most of them voiceless. But, in that silence, to listen—you could almost hear the ghostly footsteps of the departing mourners.

Our lights were lowered, once more we mounted those sixteen steps, once more we beheld the blue vault of the heavens where the Sun is Lord, but our inner thoughts still lingered over the splendour of that vanished Pharaoh, with his last appeal upon his coffin written in our minds: 'Oh Mother Nût! spread thy wings over me as the Imperishable Stars.'

PALESTINE

KATHLEEN M. KENYON

JERICHO: THE EARLIEST PORTRAITS

(From an M.S. Report)

Jericho is the oldest town as yet known in the world. Today it is a vast mud mound standing seventy feet high, and Dr. Kathleen Kenyon's expedition has put a cutting right down through all the varied layers of human occupation to the first town at the very bottom—a town which was built upon the natural rock some eight thousand years ago. These early town-dwellers did not know how to make pottery, but they had genius enough to organize themselves into an urban community living together, protected by a huge town wall and a rock-cut ditch. We know the types of houses that they lived in: how they put reed mats upon the burnished floors of their mud-brick homes. No doubt they used wooden vessels, and skins for water storage, but all trace of these have vanished with the years. Of their art we knew little until the wonderful discoveries in 1953.

In the following extract Dr. Kenyon describes the finding of seven human skulls with the features modelled upon them in clay. They are beautifully done—and Dr. Kenyon suggests that here we have the world's first portrait heads.

THE next finds were far more exciting. In the area on the west side of the mound, a portion of a human skull had, in late 1953, for some time been visible in the side-wall of the excavation. But I have already explained that it is most important that the sides of cuttings be kept straight, in order that the stratification, the lines of the floors, walls and so on, can be clearly seen. Also, it looks most untidy to have the sides of the excavation pock-marked by bits dug into them. Excavators are therefore trained not to go burrowing into the walls of the trench or square to get out objects, however inviting they look.

So the skull remained where it was until digging had stopped. But the skull of an individual perhaps some seven thousand years old is something of a special case, so one morning, after I had finished my drawing of the side of the trench, I rather unwillingly gave permission for the site supervisor to get it out. I then went off to draw a section in another area. In the course of the day the site supervisor came over with a mysterious report that the skull seemed to be covered with a coating of clay. He was told to proceed as carefully as possible, but we were none of us prepared for the object he produced in the evening. Only the photograph of it can convey any comprehension of our astonishment [Fig. 5]. What we had seen in the side of the trench had been the top of a human skull. But the whole of the rest of the skull had a covering of plaster, moulded in the form of features, with eyes inset with shells.

What was more, two further similar plastered skulls were visible at the back of the hole from which the first had come. When these were removed, three more could be seen behind them, and eventually a seventh beyond. The whole time-table of the end of the dig was disrupted. The furniture had all been packed up, the kitchen cleared and the servants dismissed, the dark-room and repair room dismantled, and most of the material packed up. For nearly a week we lived in considerable discomfort, sitting on the floor and eating picnic meals while the photographer and repair assistant did wonders of improvisation. The excavation of the heads was a very difficult and tricky business. They lay in a tumbled heap, one skull crushed firmly on top of another, with stones and very hard earth all round. Each successive group was farther back from the face of the section and increasingly difficult to get at; the bone surfaces were exceedingly fragile, and the greatest gentleness had to be used.

It took five days to extract them all, and it was a triumph of patient work to do so. We heaved a sigh of relief when no more were visible behind. But the family group of seven heads was well worth our trouble. They were all most remarkable as realistic human portraits. One was very much more beautiful than the rest. The photograph of it, still in position in the ground, never fails to produce a gasp of astonishment when I show it on the screen at a lecture. The reason why it stands out from the rest is that it alone has the lower jaw in position. In the others, the plaster representing the lower jaw is actually modelled over the upper teeth, and the heads therefore have a somewhat squat, chubby appearance. Six of the seven have eyes composed of two segments of shell, with a vertical slit between, which simulates the pupil. The seventh has eyes of cowrie shell, and the horizontal opening of the shells gives him a somewhat sleepy appearance. The state of preservation of five was excellent, but the other two were less good, one having little more than the eyes surviving intact.

Each head has a strongly marked individual character, though the technique and method of manufacture were similar. The interior of the head was packed solidly with clay, and a clay filling put into the eye-sockets as setting for the shell eyes. The lower part of the skull was then enveloped in plaster from the level of the temples, the crown of the skull being left bare. In all the intact specimens, the base of the skull was completely covered, with a flat finish to the plaster, so there is no question that they could ever have formed part of complete figures. The features, nose, mouth, eyes and eyebrows, are modelled with extraordinary delicacy. The plaster of one head is coloured to represent a fine ruddy flesh-colour; others show some colouring, but not so pronounced.

Modern anthropology provides the only close parallel for such a use of human skulls. In New Guinea, and especially in the Sipek River Valley, skulls were similarly given features up to comparatively modern times, though the features take the form of masks rather than the complete encasing of the skull. In some cases these heads seem to be those of venerated ancestors, in others those of enemies, preserved as trophies. It would be possible to interpret the Jericho skulls in either sense. I have personally always been convinced that they are the heads of venerated ancestors, largely owing to the impression they give of being portraits, and to the loving care which the skilful modelling of the features suggests. There is now some archæological evidence to support this view.

The source from which the skulls were derived would allow of their interpretation either as those of venerated ancestors or of enemies. They were found in a discarded heap beneath the plastered floor of a house. That they were typical of this phase is proved by the discovery in 1956 of two more, some ten feet away from the others, but beneath the floor of the same house. They lay in the debris of an earlier house, presumably the one in which they had been treasured. Beneath the floor of the lower house, we came upon an extraordinary number of skeletons, about thirty in a comparatively small area. From many of these bodies the skull had been removed, often leaving a displaced lower jaw. In some cases, where the bodies were very tightly packed, the bones seem literally to have been ransacked to remove the skulls, at a stage when the bodies were sufficiently decayed to allow of the separation of the limbs from the trunk, but the ligaments were still sufficiently intact for the bones of the limbs to remain in articulation. Burial beneath the floors of the houses was certainly the normal custom, but this number of burials was quite exceptional. It suggests a disaster, a plague, or a massacre, and other circumstances to which I refer below to make a massacre a possibility, though the actual skeletons show no evidence of violent death. If this were the case, it would still leave the two possibilities. If the attackers were the victors, the heads might be trophies taken from the bodies of massacred defenders, while if the defenders drove off the attackers, though with casualties to themselves, the heads might be those of important individuals, whose memory was preserved in this manner.

But though, in this instance, the evidence is ambiguous as to the interpretation to be put upon the custom, further excavation has shown that the custom was not confined to this single stage. As we have cleared layer after layer of superimposed houses in the various areas excavated, beneath almost every single floor we have found burials. In a large number of instances, the skull has been removed. The action of enemies can obviously not be invoked in all these cases. It does therefore seem probable that the removal of the skull was a general practice, and that they were kept as mementoes of dead members of the family. It is true that the instances I have described are the only ones of this phase in the history of Jericho in which we have found the detached skulls. They may have been removed to some central sanctuary lying outside the excavated area, or they might be in parts of the houses not excavated, for in no case does the complete plan of a house lie within any of our areas.

From this treatment of skulls, it may be deduced that the early inhabitants of Jericho had already developed a conception of a spiritual life as distinct from the bodily one. They must have felt that some power, perhaps protective, perhaps of wisdom, could survive death, and somehow they must have realized that the seat of these extra-corporeal powers was the head. They perhaps believed that the preservation of the skull secured the use of the powers to succeeding generations, perhaps that it placated the spirit, perhaps controlled it.

A further fascinating aspect of this find is the artistic and technical skill shown in the modelling of the plaster features. People who could do this modelling certainly did not lack the technical skill to make pottery; it can only be that they did not feel the need for it.

J. M. ALLEGRO

THE DISCOVERY OF THE
DEAD SEA SCROLLS

(From THE DEAD SEA SCROLLS, *Penguin Books*, 1956)

The story of the discovery of the Dead Sea Scrolls is one of the most exciting tales that can be told. And Mr. Allegro in the following extract gives a vivid account of the circumstances that led up to it.

'Muhammad Adh-Dhib had lost a goat.' So the story begins, in the summer of 1947. But what were these scrolls that have cost so much in intrigue and money? They were the treasured manuscripts of a sect of Jews who had retired into the wilderness and had built themselves a monastery beside the Dead Sea. For one hundred and fifty years the Sectarians flourished under their strict discipline, and then, in A.D. 68, the Roman armies swept across the land and the monastery was abandoned. Not so the library; it was carefully hidden away in caves in the wild adjacent hills, but no one was able to return, and in time the secret places were forgotten. Today scholars of many nations are poring over the texts, which include books of the Old Testament written in Hebrew, and nearly a thousand years older than any previously known.

M UHAMMAD ADH-DHIB had lost a goat. The lad was a member of the Ta'amireh tribe of semi-Bedouin who range the wilderness between Bethlehem and the Dead Sea, and he had been out all this summer's day tending the animals entrusted to his care. Now one of them had wandered, skipping into the craggy rocks above. Muhammad pulled himself wearily up the limestone cliffs, calling the animal as it went higher and higher in search of food. The sun became hotter, and finally the lad threw himself into the shade of an overhanging crag to rest awhile. His eye wandered listlessly over the glaring rocks and was suddenly arrested by a rather queerly placed hole in the cliff face, hardly larger than a man's head. It appeared to lead inwards to a cave, and yet was too high for an ordinary cave entrance, of which there were hundreds round about. Muhammad picked up a stone and threw it through the hole, listening for the sound as it struck home. What he heard brought him sharply to his feet. Instead of the expected thud against solid rock, his sharp ears had detected the metallic ring of pottery. He listened a moment, and then tried again, and again there could be no doubt that his stone had crashed among potsherds. A little fearfully the Bedouin youth pulled himself up to the hole, and peered in. His eyes were hardly becoming used to the gloom when he had to let himself drop to the ground. But what he had seen in those few moments made him catch his breath in amazement. On the floor of the cave, which curved back in a natural fault in the rock, there were several large cylindrical objects standing in rows [Fig. 6]. The boy pulled himself up again to the hole and, holding on until his arms and fingers were numb, saw, more clearly this time, that they were large, wide-necked jars, with broken pieces strewn all about them. He waited no longer, but dropped to the ground and was off like a hare, his goat and flock forgotten in a frantic desire to put as much distance between himself and this jinn-ridden cave as possible. For who else but a desert spirit could be living in such a place with an entrance too small for a man?

That night Muhammad discussed his discovery with a friend who, being the elder, was entitled to scoff at the superstitions of his junior. He urged Muhammad to take him to the spot, and the next day the two of them went to the cave, and this time squeezed through the hole and dropped inside. It was just as the younger lad had described. The jars stood in rows on each side of the narrow cave, and, in the middle, broken sherds lay amidst debris fallen from the roof. There were seven or eight of the jars all told, and some had large, bowl-like lids. They lifted one and peered in, but found it empty. And so with another, and another, until in the third they saw a bundle of rags and under it two more. If they had hoped for the glitter of gold and precious stones they were sorely disappointed, for the bundles crumbled at a touch, and, pulling away some of the folds, they could see only some black tarry substance and, below that, folds of smooth brown leather. When, later, the boys had taken this booty back to their camp, they took off all the wrappings from the large bundle, and unrolled the scroll it contained, until, as they later recounted wonderingly, it stretched from one end of the tent to the other. It seems certain that this must have been the larger of the two

manuscripts of Isaiah, the news of which was to set the biblical
world astir. However, at the time it evoked little interest
among its new owners who could neither read the strange
writing inscribed on it, nor think of anything useful to which
they could put the leather, fragile as it was. So for a time the
Bedouin carried the scrolls about with them as they pastured
their flocks and made what trade they could with their neighbours. These Bedouin have no real home. The world is their
prey and usually their enemy. This tribe has been in the
vicinity since the seventeenth century, and they have managed
to eke out a sparse enough living with their few animals, now
and again putting their detailed knowledge of the territory
to better gain in smuggling. Until the area became effectively
policed by the Arab Legion, they practised highway robbery
when they could, and always found a ready market for their
trading, legal or illegal, in Bethlehem. It was to this town that
they made regular visits to sell their milk and cheese, and
there, one market day, they took the three scrolls. Their
general dealer happened to be an Assyrian Christian, by name
Khalil Iskander Shahin, known locally as Kando, who, besides
the small general store patronized by the Ta'amireh, owned
a cobbler's shop next door. When the Bedouin showed him
the scrolls, he evinced little interest, but thought they might
serve as raw material for his cobbler's business. Later, after
they had been kicking about the floor of his shop for some
days, he picked one up and looked more closely at the surface.
The writing was as meaningless to him as to the Bedouin, but
it occurred to him that his spiritual guardians in Jerusalem
might know more about it, and accordingly, one day when he
was going up to the city, he took the scrolls along with him
to the Syrian Convent of St. Mark in the Old City. This much
is certain, but it must be confessed that from here on the story
begins to disintegrate, as love of truth on the parts of the chief
actors in the drama gives way before fear and cupidity. One
thing is certain, however; Kando began to realize that the
scrolls had some monetary value and found out that the
Bedouin had by no means cleared the cave. He and his
accomplice George accordingly launched a minor archæological expedition to the cave indicated by the Bedouin and
collected at least a number of large fragments and probably at
this time the remainder of the scrolls, making seven in all.
After they had taken all they could find, they seem to have let

the Syrian authorities of St. Mark's into the secret. In any case the Metropolitan organized his own expedition to the cave, which proceeded to ransack the place, making a large opening near the ground, and pulling out everything they could lay their hands on. Of course, it will be realized that all such excavations were and are completely illegal under the laws of the country, whether of the Mandate or of the succeeding Jordan Government. All such archæological material remains the property of the country in which it is found, until the Government directs otherwise. So complete secrecy shrouded all these operations, and much harm was done as a result. It is certain that the Syrians found some more fragments, but valuable archæological data like linen wrappings and sherds from the broken jars they threw on to a rubbish dump outside. Kando had meanwhile deposited the scrolls in his possession with the Metropolitan, on a security, he now says, of £24; and these and some fragments the Church leader began to hawk round the various scholastic institutions of Jerusalem to get an idea of their worth. It seems that one of the scrolls was shown to the late Professor E. L. Sudenik of the Hebrew University, who kept it for some time and then set about finding the rest of the scrolls, which he had realized were very old and of considerable value. He made a perilous journey to Bethlehem, for by now the Jewish-Arab hostilities had become open warfare following on the withdrawal of the Mandate. There he seems to have contacted Kando and brought away three more scrolls. This gentleman now began to get scared since he was afraid that the news of the illegal excavations would leak out, and he would rightly be held responsible by the authorities. He therefore took the precaution of burying some of the largest fragments from the cave in his garden at Bethlehem! Unfortunately, the soil of Kando's back garden is somewhat different from the parched dust of the Qumran caves, and when later he went to retrieve them he found only several lumps of sticky glue.

Meanwhile, in Jerusalem, the Syrian Metropolitan was continuing his rounds, trying to discover if the scrolls were really old. Finally, on 18th February, 1948, he called up the American School of Oriental Research and spoke to Dr. John C. Trever, who had been left in temporary charge of the establishment during the absence of the Director. He told Trever that during a clear-out of his library at the Convent,

D

he had found some old Hebrew manuscripts on which he would like his advice. An appointment was made for the next day, and the Metropolitan sent round the scrolls packed in an old suitcase, by the hand of a Father Butros Sowmy and his brother. After some hasty comparing of pictures of other ancient Hebrew manuscripts, and complicated research into dictionaries and concordances, Trever discovered that he was looking at a scroll of Isaiah, and that as far as he was able to tell, it was genuinely very old. He asked permission to make photographs of the scroll, and after some negotiations did so. As he worked he became more and more excited, for if it was as old as a favourable comparison with a photograph of a pre-Christian Hebrew papyrus fragment would seem to indicate, then he was handling the oldest manuscript of the Bible ever known. It was only with great difficulty that Trever could restrain his impatience when, half-way through the work of photography, he had to fulfil a long-standing engagement with the Curator of the Palestine Museum, then Mr. Harry Iliffe, to go to Jericho and take photographs of a local excavation. However, he seems to have restrained both his impatience and his tongue, for neither then nor at any other time was any mention of the discovery made to the authorities responsible for the control of antiquities in Palestine, who alone could have taken adequate and immediate steps to safeguard the treasures and seal the cave until a properly organized expedition could learn its secrets. Rather did Trever urge the Metropolitan to take the documents out of the country, since the situation was fast deteriorating, and war was beginning to stalk the streets and hills of that unhappy land. It was not until November of 1948, when the April copies of the *Bulletin of the American Schools of Oriental Research* reached Jerusalem, that Mr. G. Lankester Harding, newly responsible for the archæological interests of Arab Palestine as well as Trans-Jordan, learnt that eighteen months before, a fabulous discovery had been made by the Dead Sea. By now photographs of the scrolls had been examined by competent palæographers like Professor W. F. Albright and pronounced definitely pre-Christian, probably dating to the first or second centuries before our era. Excitement ran high all over the scholarly world, and in Jordan, Harding was now faced with an extremely difficult and urgent problem. The source of these scrolls had to be found, and if any related archæological

material remained, it had to be expertly examined at the first
opportunity, not only to confirm the palæographical dating
but to determine the community from whose library they had
come. Furthermore, it seemed not improbable that there might
be more scrolls, and certainly fragments, since apparently
some of the documents found were in a fragile condition with
pieces missing from the outside and edges. But the original
discovery had taken place so long ago that the chances of
finding the source relatively free from tampering were very
slight. The Metropolitan had succeeded in smuggling the
scrolls in his possession out of the country, and had taken
them to America. The Jordan Government, of course, demanded their immediate return, but by now the monetary
values being accorded them in the popular Press were so
astronomical as to persuade the Syrian Church leader that
the chances of his returning were well worth sacrificing for
the sake of the money he could expect to raise in their sale.
The one bright light in the whole miserable affair at this stage
was that he had agreed with Trever and the American Schools
to allow them to photograph and publish the scrolls immediately whilst their sale was being negotiated. The Americans
had told him, apparently, that if they were published quickly
their value would be much enhanced. In fact, it declined,
since once they were readily available in printed form the need
for the originals became less urgent. The American scholars
did, in fact, publish them extraordinarily well and quickly,
putting the scholarly world greatly in their debt.

Back in Jordan, Harding had gone immediately to the
Palestine Archæological Museum in Jerusalem, and in his
capacity as Acting Curator instructed Joseph Saad, the new
Secretary, to spare no effort in discovering the whereabouts
of the fabulous cave and any other information he could about
the find and the personalities involved. Saad's first call was to
the American School, and there Dr. O. R. Sellers, that year's
Director, immediately offered all the help in his power.
Together they went to St. Mark's Monastery, despite the
extremely dangerous nature of the journey through the Old
City, where Jewish shells and sniping were making it near
suicide to be out of doors during daylight. Slipping from
shelter to shelter they finally arrived at the building which
backs on to the dividing wall between Arab and Jewish
Jerusalem, and there interviewed a person by the name of

George Isaiah. It became clear from the beginning that he was not going to be very helpful, and, although he did not deny that the Monastery had organized an excavation of the cave, refused point-blank to disclose its whereabouts. Saad argued, cajoled, and bullied, but all to no effect, and he was just about to give up hope of gaining any useful information at all when, out of the corner of his eye, he saw one of the Syrian fathers approaching, a venerable saint called Father Yusif. When the old man had drawn quite near, Saad suddenly turned from George and asked Yusif what he knew about the cave. Before George could stop him, the old man began to describe the excavations and their whereabouts. George turned on him fiercely, but could not silence him before he had given at least a general idea of the cave's position. It seemed that it was somewhere south of the junction of the roads to Jericho and the Dead Sea, amongst the cliffs which border the Sea to the west. Now those limestone cliffs are honeycombed with caves and clefts in the rock, and the mountains rise nearly a thousand feet from the marly plateau, so that with a southern limit at Ras Feshkha about six miles to the south, a good deal more detailed pin-pointing was going to be necessary for the cave to be discovered. As Saad and his companion retraced their steps through the Old City, they discussed the next move. It seemed obvious that they would have to try the great stand-by of the East, bribery. Most things out there have their price, and it only remained to find out how high it was going to be. So on their return, negotiations with George Isaiah were opened, on the general principle that, if he would lead a party to the cave, he would receive a cash payment, and the custody of any further scrolls found would be equally shared between them. These negotiations took a considerable time, involving many trips to the Monastery through gun-fire. Finally, when it seemed that arrangements were sufficiently far advanced, Saad arranged for the mayor of Jerusalem and his dignitaries to accompany them to St. Mark's to witness the formal agreement. The party arrived on the day appointed and took their seats. Everybody asked after everybody else's health, and were asked in return, and Allah duly thanked. Coffee was passed round, and after that, the customary small talk ensued, without which no Arab meeting is considered opened. Sellers was beginning to get restless, but Saad, raised in the traditions of the East, played the game in all its formality

and was patient. At last, after the seventh round of thanking
Allah for their individual good health, the main subject was
broached, the terms stated, and nothing but the clasping of
hands remained to seal the bargain. And George Isaiah would
have nothing to do with it.

Sellers and Joseph parted gloomily at the gates of the
American School, and Saad carried on to the Museum. Weeks
of negotiation had produced practically nothing and, apart
from its general locality, they knew little more about the
cave than what had been learnt from the American *Bulletin*.
Now it happened that the Museum at this time was in the
hands of the Arab Legion, and Saad had to pass a ring of
sentries to reach his quarters. He made a perfunctory greeting
to the man on duty at the gate and then something prompted
him to hesitate and look at the soldier more closely. He was a
lean, dark-skinned Arab of the desert, of the type Glubb
always chose for his picked troops, and Saad studied his face
for a moment, noticing his long, straight Semitic nose, his
short curly beard, and black smouldering eyes. He was a true
son of the desert from the sandy wastes of the Hijaz, trained
from his boyhood in desert lore and with eyes as keen as an
eagle's. It occurred to Saad that if anybody could find that
cave, given general directions as to its whereabouts, men like
this soldier could. They would be able to perceive from an
amazing distance any disturbance of the ground round the
illicit excavations, and so detect the cave perhaps even from
ground level. The idea crystallized into a plan of campaign,
and waiting only to collect Sellers from the American School,
Saad went in search of the officer in charge of the troops in
the Jerusalem area, a Major-General Lash. He found this
officer well prepared, for only a night or two before he had been
discussing the problem with a Belgian United Nations observer,
Captain Lippens, and had that day telephoned to Harding in
Amman, asking if he would like him to send a few of his desert
troops down to the area and search for the caves. Harding
had agreed, and now, with the added information Saad was
able to provide, no further time was lost and a detachment of
troops under the direction of an English officer, Brigadier
Ashton, and a Jordanian Captain (now Major) Akkash el Zebn,
was sent down to the road junction by the Dead Sea. Deploy-
ing from this point, in such a way that as far as possible no
section of the cliffs at all visible from the littoral plain would

miss their scrutiny, they set off slowly, working their way south. Within seventy-two hours, Akkash was on the phone reporting that they had found the cave, and asking for further instructions. Whilst waiting for Harding's arrival, Ashton plotted the cave and started collecting the pottery which lay round about, making accurate notes and drawings which were of the greatest help to the excavators later. Then Harding arrived, and together they made the first preliminary excavation. Harding confesses that when he first saw the cave he was dubious of its being the source of the scrolls, but the presence of undoubtedly ancient pottery made it worth investigating further. He asked Ashton to mount a guard on the cave until such time as a properly equipped archæological party could be assembled. This was done, but the expedition was dogged by bad luck for days. Every time they gathered at the road junction it rained, which made the tracks completely impassable to their transport, and once it even snowed! Ashton could not leave his men standing about outside a cave by the Dead Sea for long, however, and it became urgent to mount the expedition, which finally started work on 15th February, 1949, a fortnight after the rediscovery of the cave. Father De Vaux of the French School of Archæology, Joseph Saad, and two others joined the excavation, and the early finding of scores of small inscribed fragments of leather, together with pieces of the linen wrappings, and the sherds of dozens of the characteristic large scroll jars, in which it was said that the original scrolls had been found, soon made it plain that this was certainly a scroll cave, if not the original one. The damage caused by illegal excavations was all too plain; no hope could now be entertained of any stratification of the remains, and some of the most valuable of the pottery and wrappings had been tossed outside onto a dump. The number of jars originally placed in the cave was now seen to have been between forty and fifty, and if, as it was then thought, each of those jars had held several scrolls, then it became a matter of extreme urgency to find the rest, which might still be in the country and perhaps suffering damage. In any case, there must clearly have been hundreds of fragments and these had also to be found and studied together, if they were to be of any use at all.

Another detective inquiry was instituted, and Saad given *carte blanche* to find and, if necessary, buy those pieces regardless of cost. It was clear now, as more and more reports came in from scholars studying the first scrolls, that every word of these documents was going to be worth its weight in gold and, indeed, that was just about what they were going to cost before they were all finally in safe hands.

Saad went again to the Monastery of St. Mark's, this time accompanied by Harding himself. The object of this inquiry was to find out the name of the dealer in Bethlehem who had continually cropped up in reports, but had never been named. If there were more scrolls and fragments about, he was the most likely person to know about them, and he would also know the names and tribe of the Bedouin who had found the cave. George Isaiah was a little more informative this time, but could not or would not describe the cave in sufficient detail to make its identification with the Legion's discovery certain, and refused to disclose the name of the dealer. Saad knew better this time than to waste much time over him. After the inevitable coffee, and inquiries after each other's health, with no more useful information forthcoming, they rose to leave, keeping their eyes open all the time for Father Yusif. It was as they were leaving the gate of the Monastery that they saw the frail figure approaching, and immediately engaged him in conversation on the cave. Unfortunately, they now seemed to know more than he, and still they lacked the name of the Bethlehem dealer. Then they had an amazing piece of luck. Harding had noticed that as they had been speaking to Father Yusif, a woman across the road had been showing keen interest in their conversation. Finally, she came across to them and spoke. Were they talking about the excavations of the Dead Sea cave which George Isaiah had organized about a year ago? Her husband had taken part in the 'dig', and had even been rewarded for his pains with a leather fragment, which the priests had told him was most valuable, although he had not yet discovered a way of converting it into hard cash. However, if they would like to wait a moment she would see if she could find him; he could not be far away. Saad and Harding looked at each other, and then to heaven. They finally ran the man, Jabra by name, to earth in a nearby coffee shop, and induced him to come along to the Museum. In the basement, the spoils of the official excavation of the cave were arranged on large trestle tables, and, bringing him near, Harding asked Jabra if he could see anything there that he recognized. The man looked long and earnestly over the

table, and then a broad smile lit his face. Yes, this. Amidst
the broken pottery and linen wrappings, the Roman lamp and
the cooking pot, he had spied his own dear, long-lost but never
forgotten cigarette roller. So another link in the chain was
forged, the cave was now definitely identified, and it now
remained to find out how much more Jabra knew. An Arab
who realizes that he has partaken, however unwittingly, in an
illegal act, is a wary creature. Harding and Saad had somehow to win his confidence, if they were to obtain the information they so desperately wanted. Bribery was of course
inevitable, and a generous tip went far towards loosening
Jabra's tongue. He admitted that they had found some scroll
fragments, and the Metropolitan had taken most of them
away with him when he left. They tackled him about the name
of the Bethlehem dealer; but at once he shut up like a clam,
and for a long time would say nothing on the subject. Harding
saw the fear of death in his eyes, and the man confessed that
he was literally scared for his life. It took a great deal of
threatening and reassuring before they finally forced the truth
from him, and when they had let him scurry off home, Saad
and Harding sat down and faced one another. Events now
had taken a sinister turn. If Jabra's fears were justified, it
meant that this dealer and his confederates were willing to go
to any length to avoid interference in their territory. It was
clear that from now on the game would be played to very
high stakes, perhaps to higher values than mere money.

The journey to Bethlehem was an adventure in itself. Today
it takes only half an hour of smooth driving on a new tarmac
road to go from Jerusalem to Bethlehem, and before the
troubles a more direct road took only half that time. In 1949,
with this in Jewish hands, as it still is, the make-shift route
was long and dangerous, a dirt track which snaked far out
into the Judæan hills by the monastery of Mar Saba. Transport was by donkey, and the journey took half a day. The
morning following the interview with Jabra, Saad set out,
taking with him two of the Museum guards, and reached
Bethlehem shortly after midday. Leaving the guards and the
animals on the outskirts of the town, he walked into the centre,
feeling suddenly lonely and unprotected. From now on he
would be working alone; any sign of official support, and
every way would be blocked; the dealer, scrolls, and everything else would go underground and nothing ever recovered.

But Bethlehem in those days, cut off from a central government by the fighting, was no place for an unprotected man to face a gang of desperate brigands, and Joseph hesitated a moment outside the shop which had been pointed out to him as Kando's. It opened, like all such eastern shops, straight on to the street, and behind the piles of vegetables and hanging kuffiyas, the bright sunlight did not penetrate. Joseph peered into the shadows but could see nothing from outside. Then he entered.

His eyes took a little time to accustom themselves to the gloom, so he did not at first see the men standing at the back of the room, watching him. One of them was rather portly, heavy-jowled, and dressed in the long Arab night-shirt type of garment, with a red tarbush on his head. His companion was an older man who stared at Joseph suspiciously from beneath heavy eyebrows, and glanced from time to time at his companion and the door standing ajar behind him. Saad realized from their manner that news of his arrival had preceded him and came straight to the point. He had heard that Kando knew something about the scrolls which had been found in a cave, and furthermore, had some of the illegally excavated fragments in his possession. There was a moment's heavy silence, and then the old man flew at him, calling him a Government spy and worse, pushing Saad against the wall as he hurled abuse at him. Joseph raised his arms to fend off his assailant, but, even as he did so, saw the other man slip out of the open door and shut it behind him. Almost immediately the old man calmed down, glancing behind him to ensure that Kando had got clear, but Saad knew now that there was nothing to be gained by waiting longer and left the shop to return to his friends. Now the fat was really in the fire. Kando knew what he was after and suspected him of being in league with the Government. The chances were that either he would try and silence Saad, or smuggle the incriminating evidence out of the country and make off, until things had quietened down. The safest thing for Saad to do would have been to make tracks for Jerusalem and his well-guarded Museum. Instead he sent his men away, and took lodgings in Bethlehem, determined to try and win his way into Kando's confidence. It was the act of a brave man.

Day after day Joseph returned to the little shop, engaging Kando in conversation at first on anything but the scrolls. He made the acquaintance of George, who appeared to be Kando's right-hand man, and had certainly co-operated with him in the illicit digging. Slowly he won their confidence, and one day brought up the subject of the scrolls again. He hastened to reassure them that no ill would come to them from working with him; indeed, if they would trust him he would find them a market for their fragments which would pay well and be perfectly safe. After all, if they tried to smuggle them out of the country they might lose everything, including their freedom. They would lose nothing doing things Saad's way. The logic of Joseph's reasoning gradually had its effect, and the first suspicion gave way to a wary, but nevertheless, genuine friendship. When he finally left Bethlehem, it was with a promise from Kando that he would come and visit him at the Museum. On the journey back, Joseph reflected rather ruefully that he had not seen a single fragment during all those days in Bethlehem; yet, on balance, he was not displeased with progress.

Kando kept his word and soon after appeared at Jerusalem, and Saad in due course paid a return visit. This went on for some weeks without further mention being made of the fragments, and Joseph was almost beginning to wonder if Kando had already sold them or, indeed, had ever possessed any. Then one day, in the gardens of the Museum, Kando took Saad over to a shady corner, looked at him hard, and then thrust his hand into the grimy 'night-shirt' and brought out a wallet. Inside, as he slowly opened it, there lay a piece of inscribed parchment, about the size of three or four fingers. Saad took the piece in his hand and studied it. There could be no doubt that the writing was very similar to that on the fragments he had already seen and the leather on which it was written was genuinely old. He replaced it carefully in the folds of Kando's wallet, knowing that one false move now could forfeit in a moment all the confidence he had built up over these trying weeks. Nevertheless, as he watched the wallet go back into its home, he wondered if he would ever see that precious fragment again. However, the game had to be played out the hard way; if Kando had that piece he would probably have a lot more, and Harding had told him to get the lot. Saad showed his interest in buying the piece and any more that Kando might have, and on this they parted, Joseph reporting the new development to Harding. In a few days

Kando returned, ready to take negotiations further. Who was Saad acting for? Joseph answered that an English Professor visiting the country was anxious to buy these fragments, but wanted more than this one piece; how much had he to offer? Kando rather warily replied that he had 'quite a lot', and arranged a rendezvous at which Saad would bring the 'English Professor' and where Kando would have all the pieces in his possession. The place appointed was to be in Jericho, and, when the date and time had been arranged, Saad went off to find the mythical financier. It so happened that, working with Harding at this time as a non-technical assistant, was an Englishman, Mr. Richmond Brown, who willingly agreed to take the part. At a preliminary meeting Harding handed over a thousand pounds in one dinar notes (1 Jordan dinar = the pound sterling), but told Saad to try and obtain all the fragments in Kando's possession for eight hundred pounds. The absolute maximum was fixed at a pound per square centimetre of fragment, but to try and ascribe any monetary value at all to this priceless material was extremely difficult. If this price seems outrageously high, it must be remembered that, at that time, the Syrian Metropolitan was asking something like a million dollars for the scrolls in his possession, and reports to this effect were being heard all over Jordan on the radio. The Bedouin and Kando were now well aware that these scrolls were considered beyond price by the outside world, and that their recovery was worth almost any amount of money. It should be also recognized that behind all these negotiations there lay the shadow of irresponsible people who were willing to buy illegally smuggled pieces for their collections or as souvenirs, or in order to make a profit on a further transaction. The danger of such loss was ever present, forcing the pace, and thus raising the price. It was bad enough that the complete scrolls should be taken from the country, but at least they could be published as a unity, as the American scholars were doing so admirably. But with fragments, it was different. They could only be made of use to scholarship if they were kept together, and as far as possible reunited with their parent documents. A small piece of Dead Sea Scroll may look very nice framed and hung over the mantelpiece, but it may well ruin the value of other larger pieces, depending for their sense on the inscription on the 'souvenir'. Furthermore, irresponsibility is not the sole prerogative of tourists and dealers. At a later stage, one world-famous museum was willing to consider buying fragments smuggled from Jordan in order to have them in their cases, even though to have taken them would have delayed the publication of thousands of others, or, at least, reduced their value for want of the additional evidence. Happily the possibility was then foiled by the more responsible attitude of an Eastern University who procured the fragments and returned them immediately to Jordan. Thus at this stage there was little quibbling about price; the main thing was to rescue the fragments and give them to the world in as complete a form and as soon as possible.

Kando's choice in hotels ran pretty low. This was a dirty, fifth-rate hovel, and, as the two drew near, Saad could see that Kando was fearing a trap and taking no chances. Lounging on both sides of the street and round the entrance were some of the grimmest, toughest-looking characters one could wish not to meet anywhere, and they watched Saad and his companion through every move and gesture as they approached. Joseph felt the thick wad of notes bulging in his pocket, and thought they could not have been more conspicuous if he had carried them in his hand. The hairs on their necks bristled as they walked in through the porch, trying to look unconcerned. Casually they asked a shifty-looking proprietor if Kando was there, and he motioned them to a room leading off the main entrance hall. Saad put his hands on the notes in his pocket, squared his shoulders, and the two of them walked in.

Kando was standing with George at the far side of the room. A table covered with a greasy cloth stood in the centre, and Saad noticed that, as usual, Kando had prepared for a quick exit with a window standing wide open behind him. It idly crossed Joseph's mind to wonder if they were as well prepared. A brief greeting did nothing to relieve the tension, and Saad asked abruptly if Kando had got the fragments. The man nodded and raised his eyebrows questioningly in return. In answer, with studied carelessness, Joseph brought out the bundle of notes, stripped off the band, and fanned them out on to the table. It was a magnificent gesture and Kando hesitated no longer but laid on to the table beside the notes a pile of decrepit-looking pieces of skin, torn and rotted at the edges, and covered with a fine white dust through which the ancient writing could just be seen. Saad passed them over to the 'English Professor' who at once began measuring them with a pocket rule. The tension had now decreased considerably, and whilst Richmond Brown was at work, Saad engaged Kando in conversation. Brown's calculations actually brought the figure to 1,250 sq. cm., but following his instructions he said, 'I can only give eight hundred pounds for this lot.' Saad looked at Kando expectantly, but the latter jerked his head and gave the click of the tongue which is the Arabic refusal. Then he began to collect the fragments together, and Saad after a while did the same with the notes. Each delayed the process as long as possible, hoping for the other to give way, but when they both had finished the silence remained unbroken. Saad walked to the door, followed by Brown, both wondering if Kando would let them go through that grim circle of henchmen with a thousand pounds in their pockets. However, they passed unmolested and started to walk towards the Winter Palace Hotel where Harding awaited them. Certainly they were alive, and had handled the precious fragments, but were they to lose them all for the sake of two hundred pounds? Harding, however, having heard their story supported their action, and was sure that the next day would see Kando at the Museum with his pieces, more than willing to sell them for eight hundred pounds.

The next day sure enough, Kando appeared. But he seemed curiously certain of his ground, and would not go below a thousand pounds. Saad said he would go and ask the 'Professor' and stepped next door to where Harding sat in the Board Room, awaiting developments. Harding agreed to the price and Saad returned and gave Kando the money. Then part of the cause of his confidence became apparent, for as Kando handed him the fragments, he looked at Joseph and said, 'And give my greetings to Mr. Harding.' Saad remembered then that, when the three of them had left the Winter Palace in Jericho that day, a bystander had stared curiously into the windows of the car. Of course, Kando now knew the secret of Saad's relationship with the Director of Antiquities, and probably realized that the 'English Professor' had been a fake. He knew too that the Government meant to deal leniently with him so long as he played their game. Indeed, Harding still had much to learn about the finding of that cave, and wanted badly to know the names of the Bedouin lads who had climbed through the hole. It was by no means certain that with Kando's collection all the fragment material from the cave had been exhausted, and there was always the possibility that new caves in the vicinity might be found any day, now that the Bedouin were on the look-out.

Eventually, Kando told Saad the names of the Bedouin and their tribe, and in due course they were persuaded to leave their desert camps and come to Amman. There Harding learned the full story of the discovery, and the Bedouin found a new friend in the Director of Antiquities. Well dined and liberally tipped, the lads returned to their shepherding to enliven the camp fires of their tribe with marvellous tales of the great city across the Jordan, and of an English official of their Government who spoke their tongue as well as they, and knew their customs and their lore better than any foreigner they had ever met. The wise administrator knows when to put the letter of the law into second place, and to the fact that Harding is such a person, the world owed much of the light which further discoveries in the Judæan desert were to throw upon this important Jewish sect by the Dead Sea.

THE BRITISH ISLES

C. W. PHILLIPS

THE TREASURE SHIP OF
SUTTON HOO

(From RECENT ARCHÆOLOGICAL EXCAVATIONS IN BRITAIN:
Edited by R. L. S. Bruce-Mitford. *Routledge, Kegan Paul*, 1956)

In 1939 was discovered the greatest treasure ever dug from the soil of England. It consisted of the splendid possessions of an Anglo-Saxon king which had been buried in his long ship beneath an earthen mound, in about the year A.D. 650. Near by is the wooded estuary of the Deben river with the tiny inlet from which the ship had been dragged to its last resting-place. Today the treasure may be seen in the British Museum.

Here is an account by Mr. C. W. Phillips of the excavation.

THIS great find came to light during the last few weeks of peace before the outbreak of the Second World War in September, 1939. A sense of imminent danger over-shadowed the discovery and spurred on the work of the excavators. In the event, seven years were to pass before its full import could be realized, because all the finds had quickly to be removed to a place of safety. For a few days the discovery was front page news, and then it was swept away by a torrent of history in the making. . . .

Before describing the circumstances which led to the sensational finds of 1939, something must be said about this part of East Anglia in Anglo-Saxon times. The kingdom of East Anglia comprised Norfolk, Suffolk and the eastern parts of Cambridgeshire, though these were debatable grounds with Mercia, and the realm is not likely to have come into full existence much before A.D. 500. Bede in his *Ecclesiastical History* (A.D. 731) records that its royal family was known as the Uffingas, or kin of Uffa or Wuffa. This man, who was probably related to the royal family of Uppland in Sweden, was the grandfather of the most famous of the East Anglian kings, Rædwald, who held the title of Bretwalda, or Overlord of Britain, for a while and died in A.D. 624-625. In describing the baptism of Swidhelm, King of Essex, by St. Cedd, Bede

E   53

tells us that the ceremony took place 'in vico regis qui dicitur Rendlesham, id est Mansio Rendili' (in a town of the King's called Rendlesham, that is to say, Rendil's steading). The little village of Rendlesham still survives at a point nearly equidistant between the estuaries of the rivers Deben and Alde, and about four miles from Sutton Hoo. We thus know that there was a royal residence of some importance close to our site, so that the presence of a royal burial ground need occasion no surprise. Further, ships belonging to the royal establishment may well have been kept on these two rivers. Since 1939 intensive research has been directed to identifying the site of the royal hall at Rendlesham. Some interesting facts and possibilities have been established, but nothing conclusive is yet known.

(*Attention was now turned to the eleven mounds on the slopes above the River Deben.*)

The largest mound was oval in form with its long axis roughly east and west. Mr. Basil Brown began to run a trench through the mound along this axis, beginning at the east end. The important fact is that, almost at the very beginning of opening this trench, and while he was just inside the edge of the barrow at old ground level, Mr. Brown recognized several of the rusted iron clench nails of a boat's hull occurring in the material of the mound in the order, and at the angle, which showed that the decayed end—either bow or stern—of a boat was protruding from the ground under the barrow. It was Mr. Brown's great contribution to the Sutton Hoo excavation that he at once saw the implication of this discovery and took steps accordingly. He rightly assumed that a boat was buried in the ground under the mound, that its length was not likely to be much less than that of the mound's longer axis, and that its keel lay roughly along this. In the event it turned out that the barrow had been considerably reduced in length, so that the other end of the boat surfaced well beyond its existing limit of 1939. No further attempt was made to open up the end of the boat, but all effort was directed towards removing the whole of the upper part of the barrow on a width of some fifteen feet on its long axis.

It was in the middle of May that the present writer got wind of these events through a hint from Mr. Basil Megaw,

Curator of the Manx Museum, that he was receiving requests for information about the Viking boat burials of the Isle of Man from Ipswich Museum. An early opportunity was taken to go to Ipswich, and the site was visited in company with Mr. Maynard. When I crossed the short stretch of heath from Mrs. Pretty's house and saw the large dump of sand that had already been moved out of the excavation I had no clear idea of what I was going to see in a few moments. When it came the sight was a shock. There, slightly adumbrated by the removal of the greater part of the middle of the overlying mound, was more than half of a boat which seemed unlikely to be less than 100 feet long overall. In the event its length proved to be 89 feet, but the first impact was staggering. I at once saw that this work ought to go no further without the knowledge and counsel of the Ancient Monuments Department of the Ministry of Works, and the British Museum, and proposed that they should be telephoned to at once. With Mrs. Pretty's consent this was done within the hour and a standstill was agreed upon. . . .

Before I took over the work it was already committed to the plan of proceeding by opening a great central trench. This was economical in effort but made a proper study of the barrow as such nearly impossible, besides creating the practical difficulty that, as the excavation deepened, two minor cliffs of sand some fifteen feet high began to loom dangerously over the main scene of work, which was at the bottom of the middle part of the boat, all of which was well below the old ground surface. We relieved this threat as far as possible by making a wide walk at old ground level on each side of the trench in which the boat lay under the barrow, and by cutting back the sides of the barrow outside these walks into outward-leaning slopes, well-fronted and retained by planks. Like much else at Sutton Hoo, this was a makeshift arrangement which only succeeded because we were lucky in having much less wind and rain than may normally be expected in an English summer.

We may now discuss the soil conditions of the excavation. It can have been seldom that, in England, work depending for its success on the tracing of decayed wooden structures has been carried out entirely in sand, but this was the case at Sutton Hoo. The heath consisted of post-glacial sand to a depth far below the range of the excavation. Occasionally diversified by a little light gravel and small rafts of clay, it was a bright yellow colour and very compact where it had not been moved at the time of the burial. This was helpful, for it was very easy to find the precise limits of the great trench which had been dug to receive the boat. The mattock strokes of the trench diggers could still be faintly seen here and there on its sides, and the infilled sand fell away from them with ease and precision, enabling us to note that the sides were vertical all round. It followed from this that the boat was lowered and not slid into the grave. An interesting point was that the site chosen for the royal cemetery was also one which had been much camped on during the Neolithic-Bronze Age transition in the first half of the second millennium B.C. Both in 1938 and 1939 pottery of 'beaker' type, which had been scraped up by their builders as part of the surrounding soil, was found in the barrows, and the marks of the fires of those who had used this pottery could be seen in section beneath the old ground surface under the ship-barrow. . . .

It has already been shown that the work of April and May predetermined the general lines which the excavation must follow. On taking over the site on 10th July it was necessary to make a clear decision how to proceed. There were already plain signs that there had been a burial chamber, and so it was determined to concentrate all efforts on studying and clearing the burial area. Only then would it be possible to make a complete examination of the boat. It seemed beyond hope that the burial would be quite intact in view of the way in which most ancient burial mounds have suffered more or less disturbance by seekers after treasure. Doubtless it would be found that the chamber had been pillaged within a few years of its completion and long before it rotted and collapsed. At Sutton Hoo we found evidences of such an attempt which, on the showing of some scraps left behind by its authors, seems to have been made round about A.D. 1600. They had given up when they reached the level of the old ground surface and found nothing, not having noticed signs of the collapsed chamber or having dug down the extra ten feet which would have brought them to the bottom of the boat and their reward. Our hope was that the chamber had collapsed before any robbery had been attempted, in days when there was still knowledge of the presence of treasure, and, most providentially, this proved to be the case.

The shadow of the impending war lowered over all stages of the Sutton Hoo excavation in 1939. There could be no delay, particularly after we became aware that the burial chamber had some contents, even though the first to be recognized were no more remarkable than some curiously well-preserved wooden wedges and some crushed sheets of thin bronze which later proved to be part of a large cauldron.

It was possible to form only a vague idea of what could be expected. Seen in retrospect it is now tolerably obvious that the best would be of Anglo-Saxon date and so, since the basic ideas behind the burial must be pagan, it could hardly post-date the conversion of the East Angles to Christianity by very long.

Thus some date in the middle of the seventh century A.D. might be expected, but at that time our minds naturally went back to the great ship-burial discoveries at Gokstad and Oseberg in Norway which belong to a period nearly three hundred years later. These burials, though robbed of their best treasures, had still contained a remarkable array of furniture, mostly in wood, but, since our site was in sand, it was clear from the earliest stages that little of this kind could have survived. . . .

By 20th July the burial chamber had been largely cleared of sand and turf infilling. The last stages of this had been a delicate business. We had now reached a point where various vague sand-encrusted forms were beginning to appear on what we knew must be the bottom of the boat, and the problem was how to advance into the area without treading on still hidden items of the funeral deposit which was obviously present. In excavation work there are often occasions on which a light, easily erected and adjusted overhead gantry device with a travelling cradle would be a godsend. Comfortable and close suspension over the scene of work free from all danger of doing damage by one's own weight is required. In the absence of anything of this kind the problem was solved by a patient, step-by-step exploration of the area from the bow end. Once a safe stance had been established inside, careful reconnaissance from this point of vantage and from the sides of the excavation showed that the plan of the burial deposit was in the form of a letter H, with the two uprights inside and parallel with the two ends of the burial chamber and the cross-bar joining them down the middle along the keel of the boat. Thus there were two practically clear areas on each side, from the gunwales down to the middle deposit over the keel.

Before saying anything about the detailed discovery and removal of the deposit, it will be well to give a quick preliminary description of its main features, to clarify what follows.

Put simply, the stern end of the chamber was the area of most importance, with all the symbols and accoutrements of royalty placed close together in a group. The chief objects were: an iron standard and ceremonial whetstone; a splendid helmet [Fig. 8], sword and shield, with the jewelled fittings of the sword belt; jewelled epaulettes for a cuirass; a set of seven assorted spears and a dirk; an exotic bronze Coptic bowl from Egypt containing the finest example of a 'hanging bowl' yet known, in which in turn were the remains of a harp; a matched set of ten silver bowls imported from the Byzantine Empire and two silver spoons, one with the name of Saul and the other with the name of Paul on it in Greek letters. Setting off from this group along the keel line of the boat towards the bow was first a group of decayed and crushed drinking-horns with silver mounts, and then a great silver dish which had been placed on the top of a pile of miscellaneous objects containing, among many other things, decayed clothing, shoes, a lesser silver dish, and a coat of mail. Finally, across the bow end of the chamber were disposed in line a great iron-hooped wooden tub and three bronze cauldrons placed in descending order of size. Near these was some complex ornamental iron tackle which is regarded as being used to hang these vessels over a fire. If any wooden furniture had been placed to fill up the spaces along each side of the chamber, it had entirely disappeared and could have had no metal elements in its construction. No sign of a bedstead was present, and the remains of sacrificed animals were entirely wanting, either as bones or teeth or, by implication, through harness or other gear.

The Sutton Hoo funeral chamber was never cleaned up with all its contents in position at one time for a single dramatic photograph. The complexity and fragility of much of the deposit made this impossible, but many record photographs were made at every stage of the work, chiefly by Mr. O. G. S. Crawford, and they are quite adequate when considered in sequence.

Objects had to be cleared and removed as soon as we became

properly aware of their presence, and this meant that much
of the gold treasure came out first, followed quickly by the
Coptic bowl and its associated objects. The work went on
swiftly with blunt bodkin, knife blade, and brushes of various
calibre. The method of survey consisted of making a well-
braced, strictly rectangular, light timber frame which was
strung to produce a reticulation of ten centimetre squares.
This could be firmly and accurately anchored to datum points
so that the relationship of the various objects to each other
could be studied and plotted on squared paper by being
observed through the overlying string grid.

The body of skilled voluntary helpers and witnesses at
crucial times of the excavation was a memorable feature of
the work. From an early stage Professor and Mrs. Stuart
Piggott were present, and to them, in the chance but most
welcome presence of Professor J. B. Ward-Perkins, fell the task
of clearing, recording and lifting the main treasure of jewellery
on 22nd July. This was a relatively easy task because of the
marvellous state of preservation of these gold objects and their
concentration in quite a small space. The only major pieces
of jewellery not found and removed at this stage were the
jewelled epaulettes and the fittings of the sword and scabbard.
To Mrs. Piggott fell the thrill of brushing the sand from the
first piece of jewellery found, one of the two exquisite terminals
of the sword knot. This came on 21st July. Hard after it came
the second terminal, and when these appeared our feelings
were as much those of apprehension as of elation, for there was
then no doubt that we had heavy responsibilities before us.
But there was no time to brood over this. If remarkable and
valuable finds were present, the conditions of the excavation
demanded that they should be removed and secured without
delay. Naturally it was the discovery of the jewellery which
forced Sutton Hoo on the attention of the world. . . .

I shall not easily forget the day shortly after the discovery
of the treasure when Mr. Kendrick first visited the site. I went
to meet him at Woodbridge station and took with me one of
the best of the small jewelled buckles, carefully wrapped, in a
tobacco tin, so that he could have an advance idea of what he
was to see when he reached the main treasure at Mrs. Pretty's
house. It was a dramatic moment when I drew him into the
waiting-room to show the buckle and the scale of the discovery
became clear to him.

The Science Museum played its part by sending the late Lt.-Commander J. K. D. Hutchison to study the ship and to carry out a proper survey of its lines with the aid of members of the Museum staff.

It was no longer possible to neglect the general security of the site when it became known that valuables were being discovered. The assistance of the East Suffolk police was sought, and until everything had been cleared from the site it was under a police guard every night.

The limits of this chapter do not permit a detailed description of the uncovering and removal of each item of the burial deposit. The process continued from 21st July, when the first item of the treasure was recognized, till 29th July, when the work was completed by the removal of the remains of the big bronze cauldrons at the bow end of the chamber. It was an arduous experience not made any easier by the number of distinguished visitors who were present from time to time and the need for meeting the requirements of the public press. Further, many of the finds were rich, strange, and difficult of successful removal.

A number of remarkable moments stand out in the memory. The first was on 22nd July, when the main treasure of jewellery was found. This requires no further comment, except that it was here that a find of the greatest scientific importance, vital to the whole excavation, was made in the shape of thirty-eight gold coins in the purse, all of them struck in the kingdom of the Merovingian Franks in France. There has been argument about the precise dating of these, but one thing appears to be certain. On the evidence provided by their presence in the grave it cannot be older than A.D. 650. Another climax was on 26th July, when the big silver dish was lifted. It was clear that this was partly covering at least one other silver vessel, and we could not guess what else might be found. As a precaution a considerable preparation was made of bowls of water, wet moss, cotton wool, and boxes, etc., to deal with any fragile objects which might appear. Arrangements were also made to photograph every phase of the proceedings, and the assorted mass of decayed cloth, pillow-down, shoes, gourd cups, etc., which was revealed justified our care. Another dramatic moment was when the great whetstone began to emerge from the sand. It was projecting upwards, and the sinister-looking bearded human heads carved on the emergent end gave it a

1. Oxen being driven past an Egyptian nobleman and his scribes for the count

THE WORLD OF MEKET-RĒ'

2. The killing of an ox in the butcher's courtyard

3. The golden effigy of the young Pharaoh. A faded wreath of flowers encircles the symbols on his forehead

TUT·ANKH·AMEN: THE WEALTH OF AN EGYPTIAN KING

4. Treasures amassed in the Antechamber, showing the three gilt couches, painted and inlaid caskets, and white oviform boxes

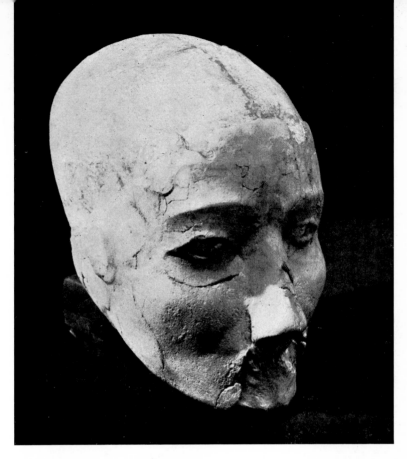

JERICHO: THE EARLIEST
PORTRAITS

5. The most remarkable of the seven skulls with plaster-moulded features. This one has the lower jaw in position (*circa* 5000 B.C.)

THE DISCOVERY OF
THE DEAD SEA SCROLLS

6. A scroll jar from cave one

7. Uncovering the long ship: the iron clench nails outlining the oak beams of the hull are clearly visible

THE TREASURE
SHIP OF SUTTON HOO

8. The royal helmet from the burial chamber

9. Stone 53 with ?17th century A.D. inscription above—IOH : LVD : DEFERRE—
and prehistoric carvings beneath

STONEHENGE: A PREHISTORIC TEMPLE

10. Aerial view from the west

11. The defences, seen from the air

MAIDEN CASTLE: THE FIRST BRITISH WAR CEMETERY

12. Roman arrow-head found in a vertebra of one of the defenders' skeleton

3. Air-photograph of a Roman villa at Ditchley, Oxon, showing the foundation walls inside a square enclosure, revealed by the growth of corn

ARCHÆOLOGY FROM THE AIR

4. The same field photographed in autumn, with no crop growing and consequently showing nothing. Both photographs were taken by Major Allen

15. Engraved shell plaques decorating the sound-chest of a lyre

A ROYAL TOMB AT UR

16. Queen Shub-ad: reconstructed head with original head-dress

17. Frieze of horses with a jumping cow

LASCAUX: A PAINTED CAVE

18. A wounded bison turns on its attacker

THE MYSTERY OF TOLLUND MAN

19. The whole man crouched, showing the leather belt, cap, and plaited no

THE BOY FROM THE LEAD MOUNTAIN
20. An Inca boy frozen in sleep

21. Wall-paintin[
the house of [
Vettiorii

POMPEII: A C[
BURIED ALI[

22. The smart [
of Verecundus,[
fashionable wea[
the Via d[
Abondanza

daunting look. The first guess was that it was a sceptre. When removed from the ground it proved to be in form a whetstone, but it is interesting to note that the best opinion now considers that it was indeed a symbol of power.

In various ways the remains of the shield, the helmet and the drinking horns were all very difficult to disentangle and remove, the latter being reduced to such a smashed pulp that the only way to get them out was to undercut and remove the whole mass on an iron plate for direct removal to the British Museum Research Laboratory, where, incidentally, two of them have been shown to have had the record capacity of six quarts.

The iron standard which lay across the stern end of the chamber against the foot of its cross-wall was also a very difficult object. All the metal was severely corroded, and, since it was built up of a number of slender rods and bars and was still essentially intact, it also had to be gently undercut and eased on to a plank suitably padded before being lifted out in one swift stroke by the combined movements of four people.

But perhaps the most odd performance was that of a large purplish lump of material about which nothing could be said except that it must be a badly corroded silver object. This also was lifted out on an iron plate and set aside while our attention was turned elsewhere. It stood quietly in the rays of the setting sun for some time and then suddenly heaved upwards slightly with a metallic click. On examination it proved to have been a set of ten matched silver bowls which had been nested together and placed upside down in the grave. In the course of time the two uppermost bowls had been reduced to little more than silver chloride, hence the purple colour, but of the remaining eight, six were in a perfect state of preservation save for some slight corrosion round the edges. Those underneath had been almost completely protected, and as the mass dried out with the overlying weight of sand removed, it sprang apart like an opening concertina.

Since the great find at Sutton Hoo had all the form and trappings of a royal grave, it was with some surprise that the excavators early became aware that it had never contained a body. The absence of obvious human remains did not of itself provoke comment, because the conditions of this grave set deep in damp sand were most unfavourable to the survival of any organic remains. But no cremated bones were found, and all the other evidence on the way of the disposition and character of the finds pointed in the same direction. There was really no room for the proper laying out of a body at the more honourable end of the grave, nor were there any of those smaller, more personal objects found which would have been on a clothed body. Chemical tests later carried out on the grave goods have gone far to prove that no body was ever placed in any attitude in this part of the grave. Thus the most remarkable burial assemblage in Britain has proved to have been almost certainly a cenotaph, and this fact has posed a nice problem for those whose task it is to interpret the results of the excavation. Theories which have been advanced to account for it include the suggestion that the man commemorated was lost at sea, that his body was lost beyond recovery on a stricken field, or that he was in fact a Christian and was buried elsewhere in consecrated ground, though family custom and public policy still required this expensive and essentially pagan monument to his memory. Here we have no time to probe further into the enigma of these pagan rites in an East Anglia which, by A.D. 650, was substantially Christian. Some of the objects found have certainly had a Christian origin, like the silver spoons, and others are capable of a Christian interpretation, but the whole taken together is still the provision for the passage to Valhalla.

When the contents of the burial chamber had been cleared it remained to study the vessel in which it had been placed [Fig. 7]. The ship has still not received the attention which is its due. This is partly the result of the lamented death of Lt.-Commander Hutchison during the war. It must have been a major vessel of its time even though there was evidence that it was well past its prime at the day of burial, and it is almost the only great example of early Anglo-Saxon skill in woodwork which has come down to us.

The problem which faced the excavators was how to body forth a faithful view of the boat as it had been when it was already known that none but the faintest traces of wood were likely to remain. Here the method of construction of the boat came to our aid. It was clinker-built from oak planks averaging one inch in thickness, and its skin had been fastened throughout by iron clench nails riveted up over diamond-shaped iron roves. Outside the area occupied by the burial chamber every one of these was still in its place relative to its neighbours, because none could move once the ship was tight buried in the grave with close-packed sand both inside and outside the skin. Thus the complete decay of the timbers affected their position not at all. The problem was how to extract all the sand from inside the boat, leaving all the nails in place and visible, and with much care and vital help from the absence of rain and wind this was achieved.

A curious fact is that, had the boat contained no metal in its construction, it would still have been possible to get a fairly accurate idea of its form by studying the pattern of old bracken roots in the sand; for wherever wood had been, there were often traces of these roots, which had followed the more nutritious conditions provided by its decay right down to the keel.

The boat proved to be 89 feet long and 15 feet wide amidships, tapering to a sharp point at each end, though it was impossible to say how these had been finished off at their extremities, or whether there had been any kind of figurehead. There was no proper keel and the boat had no arrangements for sailing, relying entirely on propulsion by oar. All deck-work and seating had been stripped out before the burial, and nothing was left in it but the ribs. . . .

The great find which has been described above raised some very delicate questions. Obviously such precious objects in silver and gold came within the scope of the law of treasure trove. It therefore followed that their legal ownership would have to be established by a coroner's inquest, and this duly took place in the village hall at Sutton on 14th August. The finds, which had for the time being rested in the British Museum, were taken back to Suffolk under armed escort, and placed in the custody of the police; and twelve Suffolk citizens had to decide whether the objects had been lost or hidden in the ground with the intent to recover, or whether the original owners had voluntarily divested themselves of their property in them. If the verdict was in the first sense, then they became the property of the Crown, which would have to compensate the finders with the full value of the collection, not as mere bullion, but as works of art. It would be for the jury to say who the 'finders' were. If in the second sense, then they became the personal property of Mrs. Pretty as the owner of the land on which they were found. On the evidence placed before it the jury had no difficulty in finding a verdict in the second sense. There could be no doubt that the placing of all these treasures in the grave was a public act and that there was no intent to recover them, whatever may have been the private feelings of some of those present at the time.

The value of the Sutton Hoo treasure has been estimated at a very substantial six-figure sum. Since in some sense the objects make up the first English regalia known, they are of great national importance without reference to their scientific and intrinsic value. Could they remain in private hands, and where would the money come from if the owner was prepared to sell them? By an act of great generosity and public spirit Mrs. Pretty solved all these problems when she presented them to the nation. The National Collection has never received a greater gift during the lifetime of a donor.

R. J. C. ATKINSON

STONEHENGE: A PREHISTORIC TEMPLE

(From STONEHENGE. *Hamish Hamilton,* 1956)

Stonehenge is the most celebrated monument of its kind in the world. No one knows how it was used, but that it was a great ceremonial building, a cathedral of the past, is without doubt. In the absence of any written record it is difficult to know why or when it was put up, but from recent excavations carried out by Professor Stuart Piggott and Mr. R. J. C. Atkinson it has been possible to deduce that building and rebuilding occurred over a period of about five hundred years between 1900 and 1400 B.C.

In the following extracts Mr. Atkinson tells us of his recent discovery, on certain of the stones, of carved axes and daggers which had hitherto escaped record. He also discusses the remarkable feat of the transportation of some of the stones from Pembrokeshire, to which geologically they belong—a distance of 135 miles as the crow flies and almost twice as far by any feasible route.

STONEHENGE stands on Salisbury Plain, about eight miles north of Salisbury and a little more than two miles west of Amesbury [Fig. 10]. To the visitor who approaches the monument for the first time, particularly from the direction of Amesbury, the first glimpse is often keenly disappointing, for the stones, vast though they are, seem entirely dwarfed by the even vaster background of rolling Wiltshire downland. It is not until one approaches more closely, so that the stones are silhouetted against the sky, that the true size of the place becomes apparent, and begins to communicate to even the most casual and unfeeling visitor something of the awe and wonder with which it has for so many centuries been invested. . . .

To the enquiring observer the signs of man's handiwork are everywhere apparent: the squared and tapering forms of the stones; the severely functional shapes of the mortice and tenon joints on uprights and lintels; and the delicate rippled fluting of their tooled surfaces, like wave-patterns left on the sand by an ebbing tide. Yet these things, though they betray the hand of the mason, and alone allow us to confer upon Stonehenge the dignity of architecture, are nowhere obtrusive. Everywhere these specifically man-made forms are being etched and gnawed by remorseless time, so that the stone, having once yielded itself to the builders and suffered shaping to their purpose, now seems to be reasserting its own essential nature by the gradual obliteration of their handiwork. To me at least this stubborn yet imperceptible battle between the works of man and of nature, in which nature must inevitably triumph in the end, gives to Stonehenge a quality of immemorial antiquity and, at the same moment, of timeless performance, that is lacking from all our other early prehistoric monuments, whose stones have only been chosen, but not shaped, by man. . . .

There is hardly a single sarsen-stone at Stonehenge which does not bear at least one inscription of a personal name or initials. One of the most deeply engraved, and probably also the earliest, is on the inner face of stone 53, a little above eye height. It reads IOH: LVD: DEFERRE.* It was while I was preparing to photograph this inscription one afternoon in July 1953 that I had the good fortune to notice the prehistoric carvings immediately beneath it [Fig. 9].

The principal carvings on this stone consist of a hilted dagger, point downwards, and four axe-heads, cutting-edge upwards. In addition there are a number of other axe-heads, less deeply cut or more severely weathered, and several vaguer markings, almost certainly artificial but too much eroded for even the most conjectural identification.

A few days after this initial discovery David Booth, the ten-year-old son of one of our helpers at Stonehenge, discovered the first of an even larger group of axe-carvings on the outer face of stone 4; and during the succeeding weeks Mr. R. S. Newall, while engaged in taking casts of these, found a number of shallower and more weathered axes on the same stone, and three quite well-defined axes on the lower part of the adjacent stone 3.

*That is, Johannes Ludovicus (or John Louis) de Ferre. I have not been able to trace anyone bearing this name in the seventeenth century, the period to which the style of lettering and the degree of weathering are appropriate. The letter E is executed in the form of a Greek Σ, an academic affectation which has misled more than one visitor into supposing that the whole inscription is in Greek.

During the same season Mr. Newall also made a rubbing
of the rather vague sub-rectangular marking on the inner
(now the upper) face of stone 57. Its existence had long been
recognized, but until the discovery of the dagger and axes no
particular attention had been paid to it, and it had usually
been assumed to be of recent date. The rubbing, however,
revealed a feature of the carving which had not previously
been observed, since it is very shallow, and has in any case
been largely obliterated by the shoes (and not infrequently
the hob-nailed boots) of generations of visitors. This feature is
a rounded extension of the upper margin of the design. As
soon as its presence was realized, Mr. Newall at once saw the
close similarity of the design to certain carvings, which occur
in Brittany in chambered tombs and on standing stones of
Neolithic date. French archæologists have termed these symbols
'shield-escutcheons' (*boucliers-écussons*), but this is merely a
conventional name which should not be taken literally, particularly as there is no other evidence for the use of rectangular
shields in Europe at the period when these carvings were made.
It is much more probable that they, and the Stonehenge
specimen, are conventional representations of a cult-figure,
possibly a mother-goddess. . . . Whatever its precise signi-
ficance, however, there is no reason to doubt that the carving
on stone 57 is of prehistoric origin. As the visitor can see for
himself, it has already been seriously damaged by the feet of
visitors in the century and a half since the stone fell, and its
future preservation is a matter of some concern. Indeed, the
only satisfactory way of ensuring its safety is to re-erect the stone
on which it is carved, or for that matter the whole of the fallen
trilithon; and it is gratifying to know that this action has been
recommended to the Minister of Works by the Ancient Monuments Board as part of a strictly limited restoration of Stonehenge. . . .

Few people who have seen the Stonehenge dagger will deny
that, once one knows where to look, it is perfectly obvious;
indeed when the sun is shining across the face of the stone, it
can be seen from the gate of the Stonehenge enclosure, over
a hundred yards away. Yet during the past three centuries
hundreds of thousands of visitors must have looked at the
dagger (to say nothing of the other carvings) without actually
seeing it. Nothing could demonstrate better that one sees only
what one is expecting to see. I do not pretend for a moment,

of course, that I was expecting to see the dagger at the time that I found it. But I am convinced that I should not have seen it, had not my attention been engaged at the time upon *carvings*, though admittedly modern ones. If these remarkable carvings can have escaped notice for so long in the most frequented of all British antiquities, archæologists may well ruefully ask themselves how many similar surprises may yet lie in wait for them in less celebrated monuments.

One final carving at Stonehenge deserves to be mentioned, if only because it forms a trap for those who care to search (and may there be many of them) for further carved symbols. On the east side (originally the underside) of the fallen lintel of the great trilithon (stone 156) is a deeply incised outline in the form of a question-mark, the upper loop of which encloses the letters LV. On more than one occasion in the past this has been claimed to be of prehistoric date, and the sickle-like form of the main outline has invited the inevitable attribution to the Druids. It has been conclusively proved, however, that this design was cut by an itinerant workman, probably a stone-mason, about the year 1829.

Having described the carvings, I must add an appeal to the visitor *not to finger them*. Admittedly the stone is exceptionally hard, and fingers are soft. But one need look no further than the recumbent effigies in Salisbury Cathedral to see what constant fingering can do; and there is no need to add wilfully to the effacement already wrought by time.

THE BLUESTONES

The bluestones of Stonehenge form two settings which repeat the plan of the sarsens: a circle of uprights within the sarsen circle and a horseshoe of uprights within the horseshoe of sarsen trilithons. They are so called from their colour, which in dry weather is a bluish-grey. But when they are wet after rain they acquire a noticeably blue tinge, especially where the constant abrasion of the feet and hands of visitors has smoothed and even polished their surfaces. . . .

The source of the majority of the bluestones has been narrowed down, by petrological identifications, to an area of about one square mile at the eastern end of the Prescelly

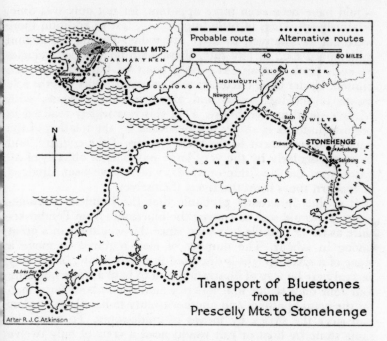

Transport of Bluestones
from the
Prescelly Mts. to Stonehenge

Mountains in north Pembrokeshire. There can be no question
of the stones having been carried even part of the way towards
southern England by ice during the Pleistocene period, and
their appearance at Stonehenge can only be explained as the
result of deliberate transport by man. The question to be
answered is therefore quite clear: by what route, and by what
means, were these eighty-odd stones, weighing up to four tons
apiece, brought from Prescelly to Stonehenge, a distance as
the crow flies of some 135 miles? Of the alternative answers
of a land and a water route, it is safe to say that the second
is overwhelmingly the more probable.

The enormous growth of rail and road transport in the last
half-century has tended to obscure the fact that carriage by
boat, either coastwise or on inland waterways, is by far the
most economical means of moving bulky material from one
place to another. The decline in such traffic (neglect of our
inland waterways apart) is due chiefly to the fact that it is
much slower than the alternatives of road and rail. In prehistoric times the undoubted advantages of water transport

F

would have been even more apparent, for not only was time, relatively speaking, of little importance, but in addition there were not alternatives, as there are today. During the second millennium B.C., at any rate, there were no wheeled vehicles or even pack-animals. The only beast of burden was man himself. Under these circumstances water transport was the sole means of moving goods, and above all heavy goods, with relative speed and economy. That this was widely realized in prehistoric times is amply demonstrated by the relation of the pattern of settlement to the river systems of the country, and more particularly by the very large numbers of objects, of all dates from the Neolithic onwards, which have been dredged in modern times from the rivers themselves.

It is thus inherently probable that the builders of Stonehenge II would seek to convey the bluestones from Pembrokeshire as far as possible by water, since this would mean a great saving in labour. The number of men required to move a stone of a given weight is discussed in detail below, but it may be said here by way of illustration that to haul a stone weighing four tons on a sledge and rollers would need about forty men for the actual pulling, and another twenty to handle the rollers and steer the sledge by means of guide-ropes. To carry the same stone by boat or raft would need a crew of only twelve men at the most, and in sheltered waters as few as half a dozen. The saving in man-power through the use of water transport is thus of the order of eighty per cent.

Admittedly the journey by water is somewhat longer than the shortest overland route, but the difference is only fifty miles. Moreover the land route is one of exceptional difficulty, for over the greater part of its length, from Prescelly to the crossing of the Severn somewhere in the region of Gloucester, it involves climbing and descending the slopes of the innumerable valleys of streams and rivers flowing southwards from the mountains of southern Wales to the sea. Even if the route kept as close to the coast as possible, a detour would be necessary whenever a river mouth was encountered, in order to find a crossing where the stream was narrow and the banks sufficiently firm. Indeed it is very doubtful whether a stone could be hauled even as far as Gloucester without the use of boats or rafts, and these would certainly be required for the crossing of the Severn. If water transport had thus to be used occasionally in any case, it seems certain that, because of its manifest advantages, it would have been used as far as possible throughout.

What then is the most probable route for the carriage of the bluestones from Prescelly to Stonehenge, using boats or rafts wherever practicable? From the source of the stones themselves, at the east end of the Prescelly Mountains, the shortest route to the sea is north-westwards down the valley of the River Severn, some of whose tributary streams actually rise within sight of the outcrops from which the stones are derived. From these outcrops to the mouth of the river at Newport is about eight miles, and over this distance the stones would have been hauled on sledges, since the stream is too shallow to allow the use of boats until very near its mouth.

In fact, however, it is most improbable that this route to the sea was used, since it involves a very dangerous passage round the western peninsula of Pembrokeshire. From Newport Bay to the mouth of Milford Haven, a distance of some fifty miles, the coast is exceptionally forbidding, with steep cliffs and numerous submerged rocks offshore; while off St. David's Head and in the sounds between the mainland and the islands of Ramsey, Skomer and Skokholm there are fierce tide-races of up to five knots, and dangerous whirlpools and eddies, to which any sensible navigator of today gives a wide berth. The distribution of prehistoric coastal settlement in Britain shows that then, too, the navigators of much frailer craft preferred at all costs to avoid such dangerous headlands, even to the point of making a portage overland. We may be quite sure that the carriers of the bluestones, borne down alike by the weight of their cargo and by their heavy responsibility for its safety, are not likely to have hazarded it, and their own lives, at the very outset of their journey.

The alternative routes from Prescelly to the sea are longer, but would make it possible to load the stones in sheltered waters at a starting-point well to the east of the most dangerous parts of the Pembrokeshire coast. There are in fact two possible routes, both leading to Milford Haven. The first follows the line of the present Cardigan-Tenby road (A.478), which passes less than two miles from the source of the stones. About two miles north of Narberth it joins the road from Carmarthen to Haverfordwest (A.40), which runs westwards to cross the Eastern Cleddau River at Canaston Bridge. The bridge marks approximately the highest point to which the river is navigable by even shallow-draught boats, for above this it soon becomes a fast-flowing shallow mountain stream.

The second route follows the crest of the Prescelly Mountains westwards to the point where they are crossed by the road from Cardigan to Haverfordwest (B.4329), and then joins this road to where it crosses the Western Cleddau River at the latter town, again at the highest navigable point. The two Cleddau Rivers flow southwards from these points for about six miles, and then unite to form the upper reaches of Milford Haven.

The existence of these two routes was originally pointed out by Mr. W. F. Grimes, F.S.A. It is impossible to say which was the one chosen, though for what it is worth the concentration of prehistoric antiquities is somewhat greater along the first than on the second. But it seems certain that in either case the stones were shipped out from Milford Haven, since the only two varieties of foreign stone at Stonehenge which do *not* come from Prescelly have both been identified with outcrops on its shores. The micaceous sandstone of the Altar Stone occurs in the Cosheston Beds on the north bank, near Langwm, about two miles below the head of the estuary; while a second variety of micaceous sandstone, known at Stonehenge from chips only, can be matched very closely at Mill Bay, a narrow inlet on the south shore, four miles lower down. The occurrence of these rocks so close to each other, combined with the fact that the estuary and its tributary rivers do form the nearest *practicable* approach by water to the source of the stones, makes it overwhelmingly probable that Milford Haven was the starting-point of the sea journey to England.

From here the next and longest stage of the journey must have been coastwise along the shores of South Wales to the estuary of the Severn. There are admittedly a number of stretches of rocky cliffs along this coastline, particularly between the mouth of Milford Haven and Tenby. But there are also numerous gently shelving sandy beaches where boats or rafts could put in, and except for this initial stage there is hardly more than five miles of coast at a stretch in which there is no possibility of landing to wait for the passing of rough weather. Provided that it was possible to wait for fair conditions (and it must be remembered that this was the universal practice of all early navigators), there is no reason to suppose that this long coastwise journey would involve any special hazards, nor even any extraordinary efforts. For the spring tides along this coast average about three knots, and the prevailing wind is westerly. So long as there was no urgency, much of the journey could have been accomplished using the wind and tides, leaving to human effort only the task of keeping the vessels far enough offshore to avoid submerged rocks and the more violent currents and eddies round the headlands.

From the estuary of the Severn there are two possible water routes to Stonehenge. The first, and by far the longer, follows the north coasts of Somerset, Devon, and Cornwall to St. Ives Bay, then by land across the neck of the Penwith peninsula from Hayle to Marazion, to avoid the dangerous sea passage round Land's End, and thence up the south coast to the mouth of the Hampshire Avon at Christchurch, and so up the Avon itself to Amesbury.

The second route, which is not only some four hundred miles shorter but also follows sheltered inland waters all the way, is up the Bristol Avon from its mouth to a point about seven miles above Bath, where the Frome joins it; then up the latter river to the town of Frome; thence overland to the head-waters of the River Wylye at Warminster, a distance of six miles; and finally down the Wylye to its confluence with the Avon at Salisbury, and so again to Amesbury and Stonehenge.

For every reason the second of these routes is to be preferred, and there is indeed some evidence that this was the route actually used. On the chalk downs which form the north-western margin of Salisbury Plain, to the east of Westbury and Warminster, there are a number of Long Barrows, the character-istic burial-places of the Windmill Hill [Neolithic] people. One of these, Boles Barrow, lies in the parish of Heytesbury about three miles north of the River Wylye. It was partially excavated in 1801 by William Cunnington, who remarked that the central core of the mound was composed of piled boulders, chiefly of sarsenstone, among which was one of 'the Blue hard Stone also, ye same to some of the upright Stones in ye inner circle at Stonehenge'. This stone, with others, was removed by Cun-nington to his house at Heytesbury, and after many vicissitudes is now preserved in Salisbury Museum. Petrological examina-tion has confirmed that it is of the same characteristic spotted dolerite from Prescelly that occurs at Stonehenge.

The occurrence of this boulder in a Long Barrow, which could well have been built at or after the time of the transport of the bluestones to Stonehenge, provides good reason for supposing that the River Wylye lay on the route. It cannot be *proved*, of course, that this boulder did not come from Stonehenge itself. But it is much less likely that the builders of the Long Barrow would have stolen it from there, in itself a dangerous act of desecration, and dragged it for fourteen miles (it weighs at least 600 lb.), than that they should have gathered it from the neighbourhood, where it may well have been discarded as useless by the original carriers after some accidental damage to a larger block.

If it is accepted that the bluestones were brought to Wiltshire by water, what type of craft was used? The alternatives are rafts, made of suitable solid logs lashed together, or true boats, either dug-outs hollowed out from the solid or composite boats formed of a skin hull stretched on an articulated wooden frame. For the sea journey the raft has some marked advantages over the boat, in that it is unsinkable and cannot be swamped in rough weather. On the other hand a raft to support a given weight is very much larger and heavier than a boat, or composite vessel of several boats lashed together to carry the same burden, and is therefore more difficult to propel by paddling, and far less manœuvrable in an emergency. Moreover, while it is possible that rafts were used at sea, it is very doubtful if they would be practicable for the inland part of the journey.

The minimum size of raft required is determined by the weight of the heaviest stone together with that of the appropriate crew. In their present dressed state the largest of the Stonehenge foreign stones is the Altar Stone, with a weight of $6\frac{1}{4}$ tons. One may assume that in its original state, before dressing, it weighed in the region of 7 tons, and would need a crew of a dozen men averaging 11 stone apiece. The total burden to be supported by the raft is thus about 17,500 lb.

The lightest timber likely to be available in quantity is pine, which when dry weighs about 35 lb. per cubic foot. A cubic foot of water weighs about 60 lb., so that floating pinewood will support a maximum load of about 25 lb. per cubic foot. The required raft must therefore contain not less than 700 cubic feet to carry the calculated load with its upper surface just awash. A log raft must necessarily consist of at least two layers of logs, one laid at right-angles to the other, and to keep its dimensions to a minimum it must be square in plan. It follows, therefore, that a raft to carry the Altar Stone and its crew, if built of logs with an average diameter of one foot, would measure 21 ft. square, with a draught of 2 ft. if built in two layers, or 17 ft. square, with a draught of 3 ft. if built in three layers. In practice these dimensions would have to be rather greater, both to give some free-board (that is, to raise the surface of the raft above water-level) and to allow for the gradual waterlogging of the wood after prolonged immersion.

It can be said quite confidently that even today it would be impossible to navigate rafts of this size along the suggested course of the Avons and the Wylye; for if the draught is kept small enough to avoid grounding in shallow places the width becomes too great, while if the width is reduced to a practicable figure the draught immediately becomes impossibly large. If such navigation is ruled out today, it would certainly be impossible in prehistoric times, when the depth of the rivers was more variable and in general shallower, owing to the existence in many places of multiple channels, many of which have today been artificially suppressed or controlled.

For the inland part of the journey, therefore, boats must have been used. What kind of boats were they? Fortunately we have plenty of evidence, in the form of actual remains dredged from the beds of rivers, for the use of dug-out canoes in Britain from Neolithic times onwards, and indeed before. It is not impossible that skin boats were used as well, though no actual remains survive. The Eskimo *umiak*, the Irish curragh and on a smaller scale the Welsh coracle are all modern representatives of the type. It need not be considered further here, however, as it is structurally unsuitable for carrying the loads envisaged.

The dug-out canoes were made by splitting a large tree-trunk longitudinally and hollowing out the interior, probably with the help of fire in the initial stages, until a one-piece hull was obtained with walls some 2-3 in. thick. The size and shape of such boats is determined by the available raw material, which is usually oak. Exceptional examples have been recorded with a total length of 55 ft., but for present purposes it will be wise to assume a maximum length of 35 ft., a beam of 4 ft., and a depth of 2 ft. The shape of these vessels resembles that of an unusually deep punt, with a more or less flat bottom and vertical sides.

Theoretically, a single canoe of this size will carry a weight of about 8,700 lb. with a displacement of half its depth. Two such boats lashed side by side could therefore support the Altar Stone and a crew of at least ten men, with a free-board of 1 ft. In fact, however, three or more boats would make a more satisfactory composite vessel. With two boats only, the load on each gunwale would be of the order of $1\frac{3}{4}$ tons, and this load would be concentrated in the central half of the vessel, measured longitudinally, so that there would be a tendency both for the sides of the individual canoes to spread or buckle and for the vessel as a whole to break its back in the middle. Three canoes, each of the same beam and draught, but only 24 ft. in length, would carry the same weight far more safely distributed. The stone would rest, of course, on bearers extending the full width of the vessel, so that the load was evenly divided between the six gunwales. These same bearers would also serve to lock the three canoes together, and if they were notched to fit over the gunwales would at the same time act as stretchers preventing the sides from spreading under the applied load.

The practicability of this arrangement was proved in an experiment devised by the writer and his colleagues in collaboration with Mr. Paul Johnstone of the B.B.C. Television Service, which formed part of a television programme on Stonehenge broadcast in July, 1954. Three 'canoes', built of elm boarding and measuring 12 ft. by 2 ft. 3 in. by 1 ft. 6 in., were fixed together by four transverse bearers and floated on the River Avon near Salisbury. A replica of a bluestone in reinforced concrete, measuring 7 ft. 6 in. by 2 ft. by 1 ft. 6 in., was lowered on to the vessel by a mobile crane. The total load, including a crew of four boys from Bryanston School, was about 3,600 lb. and gave a draught of 9 in. The crew punted the loaded vessel up and down a stretch of the Avon with the greatest ease, and it was clear that it could have been propelled, at least in slow-flowing water, by a single man. Indeed, the operation had much in common with the pleasant pastime of punting agreeable companions (built happily upon less uncompromisingly monolithic lines) upon the quiet waters of the Cherwell or the Cam.

This practical trial leaves very little doubt that some such arrangement of dug-out canoes was used for the inland part of the voyage from Prescelly. The possibility of using the same craft *at sea* is another matter, and has not so far been put to the test. There is every reason to suppose that such canoes were used at sea in prehistoric times, though not usually with so heavy a load. But in any case, as we have seen, rafts could have been used for this part of the journey, and would have some advantage over boats.

The route suggested above includes at least twenty-four miles of land transport: sixteen miles from Prescelly to Canaston Bridge, six miles between Frome and Warminster, and two miles up the Avenue (processional way) from the Avon to Stonehenge. Over these distances the stones must have been dragged on sledges.

The almost universal use of wheeled vehicles today makes us forget that sledges are not merely for use in snow, but are also by far the best way of carrying heavy or bulky goods over dry ground, where wheeled vehicles or pack-animals are not available. Indeed there are still farms in Wales and Ireland today where the horse-drawn sledge is the main, and sometimes the only, vehicle. One can safely assume the existence of such dry-ground sledges in prehistoric Britain (but drawn by men, not animals), though owing to the perishable nature of their timbers no certain example has survived. What may be the remains of such a sledge, however, were found by the writer, in a condition so decayed as to render identification uncertain, in a grave near Dorchester-on-Thames, where it had apparently been used to transport the body of the dead man from a distance. Significantly, perhaps, he belonged to the Beaker culture, to which the earliest bluestone structure should probably be assigned.

The practicability of sledging the bluestones was also tested successfully in the television programme referred to above. A sledge was made to the writer's specification of roughly squared 6-inch timbers, with an overall length of 9 ft. and a width of 4 ft., and the replica of the bluestone was lashed in place upon it. The loaded sledge was then dragged over the down immediately south of Stonehenge by a party of thirty-two schoolboys, arranged in ranks of four along a single hauling-rope, each rank holding at chest level a wooden bar to whose centre the rope was fastened. It was found that this party could just haul the sledge, weighing some 3,500 lb. in all, up a slope of about 4° (1 in 15), though it is doubtful whether they could have continued this effort for long. The sledge slid easily over the long rank grass, and left no sign of its passage apart from some slight crushing.

The use of wooden rollers under the runners of the sledge allowed the hauling-party to be reduced from thirty-two to fourteen, that is, by fifty-six per cent., and it is certain that if the rollers had been more carefully selected for roundness a further reduction to a dozen or even less could have been made. The saving in man-power is not quite as great as it looks, however, because a separate party is needed to shift the rollers as they emerge from behind the sledge, and lay them again some distance in front of it, so that there is always a sufficient number in place to form a track. Moreover as soon as rollers are used the problem of steering the sledge arises, as especially when climbing a slope obliquely it has a natural tendency to slip sideways off the rollers. To counteract this, guide-ropes were fixed to the four corners of the sledge and each was manned by two people. These ancillary tasks occupied at least a dozen people, so that the total number required to move the stone *with rollers* would be twenty-four, against thirty-two *without rollers*.

The experiment was carried out with senior schoolboys from Canford School, who were naturally unaccustomed to this particular activity; and the figures given are critical figures, that is, the *minimum* number necessary to move the stone. It seems safe to assume, however, that if the same numbers of *trained and experienced men* were employed, the stone could be moved continuously for several miles a day without undue exertion. The total required is thus in the region of sixteen men per ton weight, or about 110 men for the Altar Stone, the heaviest of the foreign stones.

There is no means of telling, of course, how many of the bluestones were transported at one time, nor how long a journey took. But for the sea and river voyage, at least, it is probable that there were convoys of perhaps up to a dozen vessels, whose crews would provide a body of men sufficiently large to ensure that help could rapidly be given to any individual vessel that found itself in difficulties.

SIR MORTIMER WHEELER

MAIDEN CASTLE: THE FIRST BRITISH WAR CEMETERY

(From MAIDEN CASTLE, DORSET. *Society of Antiquaries of London*, 1943)

Maiden Castle is perhaps the most famous earthwork in Great Britain. It has been vividly described by Thomas Hardy who could see it from the windows of his house at Dorchester. And from 1934 onwards a series of excavations was carried out there. Perhaps the most vivid episode which these revealed was the manner in which, in A.D. 44, the Roman invaders overwhelmed the place. The following is a description of the British war cemetery which was the lasting monument to the event.

AND so we reach the Roman invasion of A.D. 43. That part of the army of conquest wherewith we are concerned in Dorset had as its nucleus the Second Augustan Legion, whose commander, at any rate in the earlier campaigns, was the future Emperor Vespasian. Precisely how soon the invaders reached Maiden Castle [Fig. 11] can only be guessed, but by A.D. 47 the Roman arms had reached the Severn, and Dorset must already have been overrun. Suetonius affirms that Vespasian reduced 'two very formidable tribes and over twenty towns (*oppida*), together with the Isle of Wight', and it cannot be doubted that, whether or no the Durotriges (as is likely enough) were one of the tribes in question, the conquest of the Wessex hill-fort system is implied in the general statement. Nor is it improbable that, with the hints provided by the mention of the Isle of Wight and by the archæological evidence for the subsequent presence of the Second Legion near Seaton in eastern Devon, a main line of advance lay through Dorset roughly along the route subsequently followed by the Roman road to Exeter. From that road today the traveller regards the terraced ramparts of the western entrance of Maiden Castle; and it requires no great effort of the imagination to conjure up the ghost of Vespasian himself, here confronted with the greatest of his 'twenty towns'. Indeed, something less than imagination is now required to reconstruct the main sequence of events at the storming of Maiden Castle, for the excavation of the eastern entrance has yielded tangible evidence of it. With only a little amplification it may be reconstructed as follows.

Approaching from the direction of the Isle of Wight, Vespasian's legion may be supposed to have crossed the River Frome at the only easy crossing hereabouts—where Roman and modern Dorchester were subsequently to come into being. Before the advancing troops, some two miles away, the seven-fold ramparts of the western gates of Dunium towered above the cornfields which probably swept, like their modern successors, up to the fringe of the defences. Whether any sort of assault was attempted upon these gates we do not at present know; their excessive strength makes it more likely that, leaving a guard upon them, Vespasian moved his main attack to the somewhat less formidable eastern end. What happened there is plain to read. First, the regiment of artillery, which normally accompanied a legion on campaign, was ordered into action, and put down a barrage of iron-shod ballista (catapult) arrows over the eastern part of the site. Following this barrage, the infantry advanced up the slope, cutting its way from rampart to rampart, tower to tower. In the innermost bay of the entrance, close outside the actual gates, a number of huts had recently been built; these were now set alight, and under the rising clouds of smoke the gates were stormed and the position carried. But resistance had been obstinate and the fury of the attackers was roused. For a space, confusion and massacre dominated the scene. Men and women, young and old, were savagely cut down before the legionaries were called to heel and the work of systematic destruction began. That work included the uprooting of some at least of the timbers which revetted the fighting-platform on the summit of the main rampart; but above all it consisted in the demolition of the gates and the overthrow of the high stone walls which flanked the two portals. The walls were now reduced to the lowly and ruinous state in which they were discovered by the excavator nearly nineteen centuries later.

That night, when the fires of the legion shone out (we may imagine) in orderly lines across the valley, the survivors crept forth from their broken stronghold and, in the darkness, buried their dead as nearly as might be outside their tumbled gates, in that place where the ashes of their burned huts lay warm and thick upon the ground. The task was carried out anxiously and hastily and without order, but, even so, from few graves were omitted those tributes of food and drink which were the proper and traditional perquisites of the dead. At daylight on the morrow, the legion moved westward to fresh conquest, doubtless taking with it the usual levy of hostages from the vanquished.

Thereafter, salving what they could of their crops and herds, the disarmed townsfolk made shift to put their house in order. Forbidden to refortify their gates, they built new roadways across the sprawling ruins, between gateless ramparts that were already fast assuming the blunted ramparts that are there today. And so, for some two decades, a demilitarized Maiden Castle retained its inhabitants, or at least a nucleus of them. Just so long did it take the Roman authorities to adjust the old order to the new, to prepare new towns for old. And then finally, on some day towards the close of the sixties of the century, the town was ceremonially abandoned, its remaining walls were formally 'slighted', and Maiden Castle lapsed into the landscape amongst the farm-lands of Roman Dorchester.

So much for the story; now for its basis. First, scattered over the eastern end of Maiden Castle, mostly in and about the eastern entrance and always at the same high level, were found upwards of a dozen iron arrow-heads of two types: a type with a pyramidal point, and the simple flat-bladed type with turn-over socket. Arrow-heads occurred at no other Iron Age level, but both types are common to Roman military sites where *ballistae* but not hand-bows are to be inferred. There, then, in the relatively small area uncovered, are the vestiges of the bombardment.

Secondly, the half-moon bay, close outside the portals of the eastern entrance, was covered with a thick layer of ash associated with the post-holes of three or more circular or roundish huts. In and immediately below this ash were quantities of late prehistoric (Belgic) pottery. In the surface of the ash was similar pottery with scraps of early Roman red-glazed pottery. There are the burnt Belgic huts, covered by the trodden vestiges of the continued post-conquest occupation for which more tangible evidence will be offered shortly.

Thirdly, into this ash a series of graves had been roughly cut, with no regularity either of outline or of orientation, and into them had been thrown, in all manner of attitudes—crouched, extended, on the back, on the side, on the face, even sitting up—thirty-eight skeletons of men and women, young and old; sometimes two persons were huddled together in the same grave. In ten cases extensive cuts were present on the skull, some on the top, some on the front, some on the back. In another case, one of the arrow-heads already described was found actually embedded in a vertebra, having entered the body from the front below the heart [Fig. 12]. The victim had been finished off with a cut on the head. Yet another skull had been pierced by an implement of square section, probably a ballista-bolt. The last two and some of the sword-cuts were doubtless battle-wounds; but one skull, which had received no less than nine savage cuts, suggests the fury of massacre rather than the tumult of battle—a man does not stay to kill his enemy eight or nine times in the mêlée; and the neck of another skeleton had been dislocated, probably by hanging. Nevertheless, the dead had been buried by their friends, for most of them were accompanied by bowls or, in one case, a mug for the traditional food and drink. More notable, in two cases the dead held joints of lamb in their hands—joints chosen carefully as young and succulent. Many of the dead still wore their gear: armlets of iron or shale, an iron finger-ring, and in three cases bronze toe-rings, representing a custom not previously, it seems, observed in prehistoric Britain but reminiscent of the Moslem habit of wearing toe-rings as ornaments or as preventives or cures of disease. One man lay in a double grave with an iron battle-axe, a knife and, strangely, a bronze ear-pick across his chest. The whole war cemetery as it lay exposed before us was eloquent of mingled piety and distraction; of weariness, of dread, of darkness, but yet not of complete forgetfulness. Surely no poor relic in the soil of Britain was ever more eloquent of high tragedy, more worthy of brooding comment from the presiding Spirits of Hardy's own *Dynasts*.

O. G. S. CRAWFORD

ARCHÆOLOGY FROM THE AIR

The uses of air photography for archæological purposes were essentially a product of the first World War, but it was not until 1922 that its possibilities became widely and fully recognized, as the result of the work of Dr. O. G. S. Crawford.

In the following article Dr. Crawford has described, especially for this book, some of the ways and means whereby these discoveries were made.

WHEN I was a boy I lived in the country near Newbury, close to the North Hampshire Downs. From the garden we could see the long line of these hills stretching like a great green wall from Coombe Gibbet in the west to Beacon Hill and Ladle Hill in the east. This wall or escarpment was only a few miles from our house at East Woodhay, and it loomed up, friendly and inviting, behind every view, and I grew very fond of it. It seemed to me to have a character of its own; in one place the slope was steep and frowning above the cornfields and meadows at the foot, and could only be climbed with difficulty by some notches cut out of it, called the Shepherd's Steps; in another place the slope was more gentle, and a rough flint road led up it to an ancient earthwork or camp called Walbury, consisting of a big bank and ditch, where it ended. In those days there were (for me at any rate) no cars or motor-bikes, and I had to explore the country on a bicycle with solid tyres or on foot; the roads and lanes were not, as today, smooth and hard, but made of rough flints thrown down from a cart and left to be ground down by horse-drawn vehicles. When a lane had recently been treated in this way one could not bicycle on it and one had to get off and walk, sometimes for a mile, and it took many months to get right again. All this meant that the range of exploration was limited to a few miles from home, and that the green escarpment in the south was a formidable barrier. It was for that reason a sort of challenge, and I longed to climb the slope and see what lay beyond. We knew that there was a village there called Coombe, because three times a week an old carrier called Annetts used to pass down the lane by our house on his way to the market-town, Newbury. I talked to him and found out that the rector had some sons of about my own age, and I decided to go and call on him. I went on foot over the hill and found on the other side a great hollow in the hills in which nestled a few thatched cottages, a church and a deserted manor-house. The whole place was haunted by ghosts and they said that sometimes along the crest of the escarpment a man was seen riding on a horse and holding his head in his hands. Many of the cottages were in ruins but it was said that one could still see after dark the light from their vanished windows shining on the grass-grown track. As I returned home at night I thought of these things and was glad when I crossed the hill and got back again to the haunts of the people I lived amongst.

But I fell completely in love with the country at the back of the hills and went there again and again exploring it. On some of the steeper hillsides I found a number of flint-strewn banks which the country people (as I found out later) called lynchets [terraced field systems]. Thse puzzled me for a long time. As a countryman I was interested in the soil and plants and I had just become dimly aware of the fact that the country-side was covered with banks and other visible remains of a remote past. No one seemed then to know or care much about these things, and that made me all the more keen to examine them and find out something about them. Later on I learnt to read and study an Ordnance map of the district and found some of these remains called Tumuli marked in queer old-fashioned letters. I went to look at them and found they were round earthen mounds, and I got leave to go and dig into them. My first efforts were not very successful; then I was joined by an older man and with the help of workmen we found the burials in them with some urns and a bronze razor.

Still the mystery of those lynchets remained unsolved. Going much further afield I discovered on Great Litchfield Down a whole series of them right at the east end of the hills, just within the range of a bicycle-ride. The banks formed rect-angular enclosures, and on the very top of the downs they were so low and broad that they could hardly be seen. On the sides and heads of the valleys that ran down on the other side, however, they were very big and clear, and in places they were double as if a field-road ran between them. On the mole-hills I found fragments of gritty pottery, obviously prehistoric.

I decided to make a map of them, having just learnt how to do this, and took my plane-table up there every day on my bicycle. But it was a difficult business because the banks were so ill-defined, and eventually I gave up the attempt. Then the First World War broke out and I had to take part in it, rather unwillingly, because there were so many much more interesting things to do. However, it became more exciting when the first aeroplane went up and took the first air-photographs. I thought of my recent efforts on Great Litchfield Down and how much easier it would be to see a place by just going up in an aeroplane and taking a photograph of the area. It was not the first time I had had this idea, for already before the war I had told a friend, Dr. Williams-Freeman, about these banks, now called Celtic or prehistoric fields, and we had wished that we could go up in an aeroplane and see them properly. There were many other things besides these fields which we agreed we could see better from the air. There were those long grass-ditches (now called ranch-boundaries or bivallates, because they usually had a bank-vallum on each side). These were plain enough on the open downs, but when in their course they reached ploughed fields they had been levelled, but could still be seen—from a height or a distance—because the corn grew greener over the silted-up ditch, and the banks showed up as white chalky bands on each side. We realized that from the air one would be able to trace the course of these ditches quite plainly through cultivated land that one could not traverse on foot because of the corn. In the days before the war flying was impossible for ordinary people and it was not very easy even after it, and in any case I had other things to do. I did try to get access to air-photographs taken over the downs, but it was difficult then to do so for military reasons, and the people I approached were not interested.

One day, in or about 1922, Dr. Williams-Freeman, who lived and practised at Weyhill near Andover, told me that an R.A.F. friend of his, Air-Commodore Clark-Hall, who was stationed on the adjacent aerodrome, had shown him some air-photographs taken in the district which had queer markings on them, and he invited me to go and stay with him and see them. Clark-Hall suspected that the marks were indications of something archæological, and had shown them to Williams-Freeman whom he knew to be interested in such matters. I well remember the occasion; Clark-Hall brought out his photo-

G

graphs and showed them to us in his office. They were covered
with rectangular white marks which at once recalled to my
mind the ones I had started to map on Great Litchfield Down
nearly ten years before. Here in these few photographs was
the answer to the problem, but it was much more than that.
The photographs also showed *dark* lines which were obviously
silted-up ditches revealed by the darker growth of corn, which
grew better (and therefore had a darker green colour) than
the rest. There were also some areas of downland that had
not been ploughed since these early fields, with their lynchets,
had been finally abandoned some 1,600 years ago. I realized
that air-photography was going to be of enormous help to
archæologists in unravelling the marks of all kinds left in the
ground and above it by prehistoric man. It was quite a
dramatic revelation, for at that very moment I knew that a
new technique had been found, and that thanks to my having
a post as Archæology Officer at the Ordnance Survey I had
the means of developing that technique and making it available
to the world at large. One did not have to fly one's self; all
that was necessary was to transfer those marks to the large
scale Ordnance map, and one would then have a plan of the
actual fields as they were at the time they were in use. It must
be remembered that at that time the very *existence* of those
fields was practically unknown, though a few countrymen had
seen the lynchets and recognized what they were.

I set to work and had the marks transferred to the map.
There was nothing difficult in doing this; we had done the
same with the German trenches during the war. When this had
been done I checked some of the marks by ground inspection
and gave an account of the whole affair in a lecture delivered
before the Royal Geographical Society in London. That
lecture was quite an occasion, and I felt that many of those
present felt, as I did, that they were gazing, as from 'a peak
in Darien', upon a whole new world of the past that was now
opening for exploration.

The next thing to do was to get hold of as many air-photographs as possible and examine them for other marks, most of
which would probably represent new discoveries. So (after the
necessary authority had been obtained) I collected negatives
that were no longer required by the R.A.F., particularly some
stored on the aerodrome at Old Sarum, and these formed the
nucleus of a collection deposited at the Ordnance Survey. I

used to look rapidly over these negatives at the aerodrome in order to select those that seemed to be most 'meaty', and it was while doing this that I found, on one or two of those taken near Stonehenge, a pair of dark parallel lines that continued the line of the Stonehenge Avenue across ploughed fields where it had disappeared. Soon afterwards I verified this by digging, and found that the dark lines, caused by the growth of corn, marked the course of the ditch; for that Avenue consists of a bank and a ditch about seventy feet apart, running from Stonehenge north-eastwards and then eastwards. Everyone has heard of Stonehenge, and every discovery about it is news; so this find actually had greater publicity than my original one of the prehistoric fields.

What neither Dr. Williams-Freeman nor I realized before we saw those first archæological air-photographs was the startling sharpness and clearness of the various markings; they were no mere vague smudge but sharply defined bands of light and dark. Later on I was able to fly myself and see these things directly below me with my own eyes. One of the commonest objects is the dark circular rings that represent the ditches round barrows, the burial-mounds of the Bronze Age. There are a great many of them and they catch the eye at once, even if one is not in the least interested in archæology. Professional pilots have told me that they see them often during their flights—or used to before they flew too quickly to see anything but their cockpits. These sites revealed by vegetation are called 'crop-sites', and it is by such means that the most important new discoveries have been made, for normally it is impossible to see anything at all in the ground. The image or pattern is not, indeed, in the ground but in the corn, and it vanishes in winter. The top of the corn is too high for a person standing beside it to see anything, though sometimes, when one is used to the job, one can see a sort of blur which one suspects to be something interesting, but it may be merely where the manure was more abundant.

You will remember that those banks on Great Litchfield Down which I tried to map were difficult to see at all because they were very low and broad. They are also difficult to see from the air for the same reason except at certain times. When the sun is low and shines at right-angles to them they cast a shadow, or more accurately, one side of the low slope is in shadow and darker than the other side. At sunrise and sunset these field-systems are seen as clearly as if the fields were still in use. When I was flying over Salisbury Plain in 1924 I used to do the first flight before breakfast; then the whole of the plain was covered with patches of these fields, and we used to say that that hour after dawn (and before sunset) was 'lynchet-time'. But when I flew back only an hour or so later they had all vanished completely; it was quite remarkable how a very slight difference in the sun's height above the horizon was enough to cause the shadow—and the fields—to disappear. It was in exactly the same way that Atkinson found the axes carved on Stonehenge; except that here the marks were not raised but sunken. The axes are practically invisible at most times, but when the sun comes round and shines on that side of the stone they become visible with dramatic suddenness. It is a sudden, not a gradual, process, occupying a few minutes only; I remember vividly how I saw it happen while I was waiting for the sun to come round so that I might photograph the axes.

Of course this new technique of air-archæology soon became quite famous; it had some of the romance attached in the early days to flying itself. The fact that air-photography revealed things that were not previously known made some people think that the camera itself had some magic power, enabling it to see what was invisible to the human eye. That of course is not so; the camera sees no more and no less than you or I could if we had time to look carefully while flying over a site. It is the point of view, *above* the object, that makes it possible to see these things properly, as on a plan—and of course it is *plans* that we always use in archæology. I once explained the difference between what one sees on the ground and what one can see from the air as the difference between the cat's view of the carpet and ours. The cat, curled up before the fire, is too close to the carpet to see the pattern, nor could you if you lay down and put your head on the floor. But standing up you can see the pattern perfectly; you are like the man in the aeroplane looking down from a height at the pattern of pre-historic fields below.

This technique of air-photography, then, works mainly by means of crop-sites and shadow-sites [Figs. 13, 14]; a third variety is soil-sites, such as those white rectangular marks that first revealed the Hampshire fields. To get results you have to study the local conditions and take photographs at the right time of day and year. It is no use looking for crop-sites in mid-winter or shadow-sites at midday. On the other hand, when there is a long drought you can find crop-sites in grass fields where at other times there is nothing to be seen, because the grass does not burn brown over ditches and pits. Why? Because they are full of soil which retains the moisture. Conversely, grass or corn growing over the hard stony causeway of a Roman (or any other matalled) road burns up quickly and withers, and from the air shows up as a broad light band. In the Roman town of VRICONIVM (Wroxeter, near Shrewsbury) the whole plan of the streets and houses is revealed as a vast crop-site, but the mosaic pavements in the houses, impenetrable by roots, appear to be white patches on the photographs. Other effects are produced by a light fall of snow, drifting, or melting, at an uneven rate over disturbed and undisturbed ground. Occasionally, as in the Fens, floods will reveal ancient village sites and embanked water-channels.

Since I first began to develop this new technique in this country many others have come along and carried it much further, both here and abroad. In England pioneer work was first done by Squadron Leader Insull who discovered Wood-henge near Stonehenge and Seleucia near Baghdad. The finest work of all was done by George Allen during the 1930's; you can see enlargements of his photographs admirably displayed in the Ashmolean Museum at Oxford. During and after the war a whole new field was opened up in Italy by John Bradford who found a vast number of entrenched Neolithic villages, cultivated Roman fields, and later medieval ones. Abroad, the French, following our lead, have done good work in Syria and North Africa. But there is still a huge field to be covered, and opportunities for anyone who takes the trouble to learn the technique to make exciting new discoveries.

AFRICA

A. MERLIN

ARCHÆOLOGY FROM THE SEA:
THE MAHDIA WRECK

(From LES FOUILLES SOUS-MARINES DE MAHDIA. *Tunis*, 1911)

This is an account of one of the first underwater excavations. Monsieur Merlin, then Head of the Department of Antiquities at Tunis, tells of the hopes and fears and difficulties of the team who salvaged works of art and architecture from the wreck of a ship, which foundered about two thousand years ago and which lay in deep and dangerous water off the African coast.

Many of the beautiful things that were brought to the surface can be seen today in the Bardo Museum at Tunis.

Ladies and Gentlemen,

YOU have all surely heard of the underwater excavations at Mahdia; you know that to the east of Tunis, between Sousse and Sfax, the remains of an ancient wreck have been found. But perhaps you do not know the way in which the exploration was carried out at the bottom of the sea, and the nature and interest of the objects that were salvaged. Where was the ship coming from and where was it going to when disaster overtook it? I propose to tell you something of the story of this richly laden vessel which was carrying works of art, furniture, and building materials, all snatched from Athens and bound for Italy; how the ship foundered on the inhospitable coast by Syrtes at the beginning of the first century B.C.; and how we, two thousand years later, have been able to retrieve this treasure.

The discovery was made by sponge-fishers. In June 1907, some Greek divers were working in the vicinity of Mahdia, and one of them returned to the surface with a strange tale. He declared that he had seen a 'row of big cannons' lying in the mud. There was great speculation among the crew and the captain decided to spend a little time investigating the area. It was then that the wreck was found. Since then the Antiquities Department has taken charge and has carried out the excavations which have produced outstanding and important results. The objects that have been found are of high artistic quality, but an added interest comes from the fact that they were salvaged from the sea, and that is why, before I give you an account of the works of art themselves, I will tell you something of the manner in which the exploration was carried out. I will tell you of the difficulties and attempt to make you share the hopes and fears of those concerned in this deep-sea catch.

We are now at Mahdia. It is early morning of a summer's day, and we board one of the Greek sponge-fishers' boats which unfurls its huge sail. Leaving the port, we pass the Arab quarter and the lighthouse as we round the headland along which the small town has sprawled. With a good wind we shall have yet an hour's sailing, but without it we must put out the great oars and toil for three long hours for we must make our way some five kilometres to the NE. of the Point. We cannot guarantee a calm sea for there is always the chance of rough weather and the Mediterranean hereabouts justifies Sallust's comment—a 'terrible' sea. The trip is hard on those who are not good sailors because these boats toss and pitch in any water. But when there is a high wind blowing it is unsafe to venture past the protecting arm of the promontory and we cannot work on such a day.

Little by little we approach the spot; and we can see the marking buoy. Sometimes during the night gales have torn it away and we have had to begin again to locate the wreck by using fixed points from the shore. It is a laborious business— but happily such tiresome time-wasters occur rarely. We throw the anchor overboard and the day's work begins.

Our boat carries a team of divers. Some of them leisurely await their turn in the stern of the ship; others prepare themselves in the bow for the descent, and the leader holds the line to which each diver in his turn is attached. Amidships is the airpump which is worked by hand. Already one diver has come up and another puts on his helmet and climbs overboard. Now we can only follow him in imagination.

Weighted with small packets of lead strapped to his back and chest he sinks for a long time, because here the depth is about 120 feet, the height of two six-storey houses, one on top of the other.

When at last he gets to the bottom he is confronted with a great mass of columns (there are sixty in all) and they lie side by side in six rows. The shafts of the columns are not all of equal length but they have been placed in continuous lines that stretch from north to south for 96 feet. Pieces of marble are scattered about in profusion, as well as capitals and bases of columns, carefully squared blocks and architectural fragments. Among all this material, especially at the northern end of the ship, there are innumerable broken pots, all that remains of earthenware vessels that had been stacked aboard: cracked and broken amphorae, jars of all kinds that had contained oil, wine, water, foodstuffs, and other things needed by the crew during the voyage. At the southern end of the ship are enormous masses of lead—one piece we were able to haul up weighed as much as 600 kilos. These leaden bars constituted the remains of the anchors which had been in the bow. But all that I have told you so precisely appeared far less distinctly as originally found. At first it seemed just to be a *mélange* of columns, blocks of marble, amphorae and anchors, all buried in the mud.

In order to get our results it was necessary to remove all obstructions and to dig away the cloak of covering mud. There was no easy way of lifting the columns, for the shafts were, on an average, twelve feet long and twenty-five inches in diameter. To dig them out the diver has to stir up the mud which constantly permeates the water and envelops everything in an opaque gloom. He kneels there on the sea-bed working with his hands, in the faint glimmer of light which penetrates to this depth. Slowly he makes a tunnel under some object through which he can pass a rope to haul it aside, or if it is a good piece to drag it into position for raising. At certain times his task is very gruelling, and even dangerous, because not only is he subject to the severe pressure of the water above him but there is often an icy current, against which he must battle all the time in order to retain his place.

When the men manage to dig under or between certain of the columns, they come across an eighteen-inch layer of partially decomposed wood. This had once been the deck, and below this they find the delicate objects which had been stowed away in the holds. Here, there are fine statuettes in bronze and pieces of furniture with graceful inlay. It seems clear that the ship, when she foundered, must have gone straight to the bottom without turning turtle or breaking up, and that for the two thousand years which followed not only has she been supported by mud, but many of the objects have been protected from damage and corrosion in this firm bed of slime.

Each diver trained to work at such depths is able to stay below for thirty or forty minutes, after which he comes to the surface bringing with him anything that he has been able to retrieve from the wreck. It is an exciting moment for those waiting above, where time seems endless while the diver is at his work below. You must not think that each time a diver returns he is able to bring a masterpiece to the surface—sometimes he only clutches a fragment from the ship, oxidized nails, wood, bits of lead. And often whole days pass and we find nothing worthwhile. But there are the occasions when the chief diver, hauling a comrade upwards, feels a heavier weight on the rope and we all wonder what it can be. Perhaps it is a bronze statuette. Should this be so, no matter how formless it may appear, covered with slime and marine deposit, we all feel that our labours have been rewarded and we forget our exhaustion and continue with renewed enthusiasm.

Once the objects have been extracted they are cleaned—we remove the dense crust of shellfish and marine deposit that envelops them and makes them almost unrecognizable. We piece together the fragments: arms and legs have sometimes been found months later, bits of furniture must be joined together and it is sometimes possible to identify the decorative inlay from the pattern that has been left on metal. Thus, thanks to minute and complicated work, we are able to restore many of the objects to their original shape and, in spite of the damage caused by twenty centuries at the bottom of the sea, we can appreciate their artistic value and obtain an important and documentary picture of those far-off times. . . .

But I hasten to come to the question that you must be asking yourselves: whence did this cargo come and where was it going when disaster overtook the ship?

All these works of art in marble and bronze, all these building materials and pieces of furniture, came from Athens. We have found inscribed Greek slabs, one of which is a decree issued by the Paroloi, the citizens of Athens who formed the crew of the trireme Parolos which was one of the two Sacred Ships; others are dedication stones from the shrines of Piræus. Without doubt it was from the arsenal at Piræus that two huge bronze cornices, adorned with the heads of Dionysos and Ariadne, were wrenched away. It is from the temple of

Asklepios at Piræus, too, that the ex-voto offering must come which shows the figure of the god reclining on a couch in front of a table laden with food, with his daughter Hygieia seated by him. They are attended by a serving-man and a number of worshippers.

Some of the capitals, decorated on either face with gryphons' heads and two curled wings, take us back again to Athens. The type is very rare, not only on our ship, where most of the capitals are Ionic, but in the ancient world, types such as these appear in two buildings only: a tomb at Pompeii where most probably they are imports, and the theatre of Dionysos at Athens. The white heavily veined marble from which the columns, capitals and statues are cut could have come only from Hymettus.

Our ship then, set out from Athens, but in order to know where she was going let us first establish the date.

The earliest date that we have so far is given by the Hermes of Boëthos, which cannot be earlier than the beginning of the second century B.C., but we have another object of fixed date which is a terracotta lamp, salvaged with its charred wick *in situ* and obviously part of the ship's furniture. This lamp is characteristic of the end of the second century B.C. and could have still been in use in the early years of the first. For the rest, if our ship carried inscribed stones from the sanctuaries of the Piræus, the journey must have been made after the taking of Piræus by Sulla in 86 B.C. It was then that the arsenal and storehouses were sacked and burnt and the temples desecrated.

Since there are no objects of a later date it appears that the voyage and wreck took place shortly after the capture of the town by Sulla.

But where was the cargo being taken to? There was no person or town of sufficient importance in Africa at this time to have been in a position to have commanded such treasures. If the ship sank off the coast of Syrtes it was not because it was about to put in there but because it had been driven there by storms. The ship was probably going to Italy, to the Campagna, or more likely, to Rome. This is a suggestion which cannot be substantiated but it is in accordance with all that we know of the tastes of the Romans at that time. Sulla himself ordered Athenian columns to be re-used when the Capitol was rebuilt after the great fires of the Civil War in 83 B.C., and Lucian

reminds us of a ship, loaded with works of art, sent to Rome
by Sulla from Athens which sank after rounding Cape Malea.
This example is significant and curiously like our own. Typical
too of those times are these extracts from Cicero's letters to his
friend Atticus, who was in Athens in 67-66 B.C. (a date near
the time of our wreck). Cicero writes: 'I was glad to learn
that you had bought me some statues of Hermes in Pentelic
marble. Send them to me as quickly as possible. I want to
have them at once.' Or: 'I have received the statue in Megara
marble that you sent me. It is beautiful and I will have it in
my villa at Tusculum. If you find any other suitable statuary,
do not hesitate to buy it for me.' And some years later he went
to considerable trouble to procure columns for his daughter
Tullia's tomb.

In fact, during the next few years, ships were constantly
leaving Athens bound for Italy, bearing away works of art and
columns for public buildings, private houses and villas, for the
adornment of porticos and gardens, and for the furnishing of
staterooms and banqueting halls.

Could we want better comparisons? The columns from our
wreck would adorn any building, as would the statues and
candelabra. Our statuettes would please the eye with their
elegance or bring a smile to the lips with their lively caricature.
We have found furniture to grace salons and inscriptions to
please the man of letters.

Is it not legitimate then to suppose that ours was one of
those ships carrying loot to Rome, and that the cargo was
composed of the spoil of Athens and Piræus.

But those who awaited the arrival of our ship carrying their
treasures had not thought of the hazards of the crossing or the
dangers of the sea by Syrtes. Battered by gales, the ship was
driven towards the African coast, and, being too heavily
loaded to ride out the storm, sank, taking with her the precious
cargo.

It is possible that the ship sailed under bad auspices, that it
had been cursed by the gods whose altars had been despoiled.
And if, after more than nineteen hundred years we, here in
Africa, have inherited the works of art intended by Rome for
the glorification of the Republic, perhaps it is those same gods,
in a moment of anger, who wish still to be revenged on Rome
by enriching Carthage and the soil of Africa at Rome's expense.

IRAQ

SIR LEONARD WOOLLEY

A ROYAL TOMB AT UR

(From EXCAVATIONS AT UR. *Ernest Benn*, 1954)

The famous city of Ur, the city of Abraham, is today a tumbled patch of desert near the Euphrates in Southern Iraq. At one time, five thousand years ago and more, it was populous and wealthy. In its midst a high terraced platform or 'ziggurat' bore aloft the principal temple of the place, counterpart to the great tower at Babylon which we know as the 'Tower of Babel'. Farmers, traders, craftsmen, all contributed to the busy and picturesque life of the city which was dominated by priestly rulers with their varied ritual.

In 1927, Sir Leonard Woolley, digging deeply below the present surface, came upon tombs so dramatically rich that they must have contained either members of the royal family or ritual burials of similarly exalted status. In the following extract Sir Leonard Woolley describes his macabre discoveries in one of these tombs dating from about 2600 B.C.

IN that season, 1927-8, digging in another part of the cemetery area, we came upon five bodies lying side by side in a sloping trench; except for the copper daggers at their waists and one or two small clay cups they had none of the normal furniture of a grave, and the mere fact of there being a number thus together was unusual. Then, below them, a layer of matting was found, and tracing this along we came to another group of bodies, those of ten women carefully arranged in two rows; they wore head-dresses of gold, lapis lazuli, and carnelian, and elaborate bead necklaces, but they too possessed no regular tomb furnishings. At the end of the row lay the remains of a wonderful harp, the wood of it decayed but its decoration intact, making its reconstruction only a matter of care; the upright wooden beam was capped with gold, and in it were fastened the gold-headed nails which secured the strings; the sounding-box was edged with a mosaic in red stone, lapis lazuli and white shell, and from the front of it projected the splendid head of a bull wrought in gold with eyes and beard of lapis lazuli; across the ruins of the harp lay the bones of the gold-crowned harpist.

By this time we had found the earth sides of the pit in which the women's bodies lay and could see that the bodies of the five men were on the ramp which led down to it. Following the pit along, we came upon more bones which at first puzzled us by being other than human, but the meaning of them soon became clear. A little way inside the entrance to the pit stood a wooden sledge chariot decorated with red, white, and blue mosaic along the edges of the framework and with golden heads of lions and bulls, silver lionesses' heads adorned the front, and the position of the vanished swingletree was shown by a band of blue and white inlay and two smaller heads of lionesses in silver. In front of the chariot lay the crushed skeletons of two asses with the bodies of the grooms by their heads, and on the top of the bones was the double ring once attached to the pole, through which the reins had passed; it was of silver, and standing on it was a gold 'mascot' in the form of a donkey, most beautifully and realistically modelled.

Close to the chariot were an inlaid gaming-board and a collection of tools and weapons, including a set of chisels and a saw made of gold, big bowls of grey soap-stone, copper vessels, a long tube of gold and lapis which was a drinking-tube for sucking up liquor from the bowls, more human bodies, and then the wreckage of a large wooden chest adorned with figured mosaic in lapis lazuli and shell which was found empty but had perhaps contained such perishable things as clothes. Behind this box were more offerings, masses of vessels in copper, silver, stone (including exquisite examples in volcanic glass, lapis lazuli, alabaster, and marble), and gold; one set of silver vessels seemed to be in the nature of a communion-service, for there was a shallow tray or platter, a jug with tall neck and long spout such as we know from carved stone reliefs to have been used in religious rites, and tall slender silver tumblers nested one inside another; a similar tumbler in gold, fluted and chased, with a fluted feeding-bowl, a chalice, and a plain oval bowl of gold lay piled together, and two magnificent lions' heads in silver, perhaps the ornaments of a throne, were amongst the treasures in the crowded pit. The perplexing thing was that with all this wealth of objects we had found no body so far distinguished from the rest as to be that of the person to whom all were dedicated; logically, our discovery, however great, was incomplete.

The objects were removed and we started to clear away the remains of the wooden box, a chest some six feet long and three feet across, when under it we found burnt bricks. They had fallen, but at one end some were still in place and formed the ring-vault of a stone chamber. The first and natural supposition was that here we had the tomb to which all the offerings belonged, but further search proved that the chamber was plundered, the roof had not fallen from decay but had been broken through and the wooden box had been placed over the hole as if deliberately to hide it. Then, digging round the outside of the chamber, we found just such another pit as that six feet above. At the foot of the ramp lay six soldiers, orderly in two ranks, with copper spears by their sides and copper helmets crushed flat on the broken skulls; just inside, having evidently been backed down the slope, were two wooden four-wheeled wagons each drawn by three oxen—one of the latter so well preserved that we were able to lift the skeleton entire; the wagons were plain, but the reins were decorated with long beads of lapis and silver and passed through silver rings surmounted with mascots in the form of bulls; the grooms lay at the oxen's heads and the drivers in the bodies of the cars; of the cars themselves only the impression of the decayed wood remained in the soil, but so clear was this that a photograph showed the grain of the solid wooden wheel and the grey-white circle which had been the leather tyre.

Against the end wall of the stone chamber lay the bodies of nine women wearing the gala head-dress of lapis and carnelian beads from which hung golden pendants in the form of beech leaves, great lunate ear-rings of gold, silver 'combs' like the palm of a hand with three fingers tipped with flowers whose petals are inlaid with lapis, gold, and shell, and necklaces of lapis and gold; their heads were leaned against the masonry, their bodies extended on to the floor of the pit, and the whole space between them and the wagons was crowded with other dead, women and men, while the passage which led along the side of the chamber to its arched door was lined with soldiers carrying daggers, and with women. Of the soldiers in the central space, one had a bundle of four spears with heads of gold, two had sets of four silver spears, and by another there was a remarkable relief in copper with a design of two lions trampling on the bodies of two fallen men which may have been the decoration of a shield.

On top of the bodies of the 'court ladies' against the chamber wall had been placed a wooden harp, of which there survived only the copper head of a bull and the shell plaques which had adorned the sounding-box; by the side wall of the pit, also set on the top of the bodies, was a second harp with a wonderful bull's head in gold, its eyes, beard, and horn-tips of lapis, and a set of engraved shell plaques not less wonderful; there are four of them with grotesque scenes of animals playing the parts of men, and while the most striking feature about them is that sense of humour which is so rare in ancient art, the grace and balance of the design and the fineness of the drawing make of these plaques one of the most instructive documents that we possess for the appreciation of the art of early Sumer [Fig. 15].

Inside the tomb the robbers had left enough to show that it had contained the bodies of several minor people as well as that of the chief person, whose name, if we can trust the inscription on a cylinder seal, was A-bar-gi; overlooked against the wall we found two model boats, one of copper now hopelessly decayed, the other of silver wonderfully well preserved; some two feet long, it has a high stern and prow, five seats, and amidships an arched support for the awning which would protect the passenger, and the leaf-bladed oars are still set in the thwarts; it is a testimony to the conservatism of the East that a boat of identical type is in use today on the marshes of the Lower Euphrates, some fifty miles from Ur.

The king's tomb-chamber lay at the far end of this open pit; continuing our search behind it we found a second stone chamber built up against it, either at the same time or, more probably, at a later period. This chamber, roofed like the king's with a vault of ring arches in burnt brick, was the tomb of the queen to whom belonged the upper pit with its chariot and other offerings: her name, Shub-ad, was given us by a fine cylinder seal of lapis lazuli which was found in the filling of the shaft a little above the roof of the chamber and had probably been thrown into the pit at the moment when the earth was being put back into it. The vault of the chamber had fallen in, but luckily this was due to the weight of earth above, not to the violence of tomb-robbers; the tomb itself was intact.

At one end, on the remains of a wooden bier, lay the body of the queen, a gold cup near her hand; the upper part of the body was entirely hidden by a mass of beads of gold, silver,

lapis lazuli, carnelian, agate, and chalcedony, long strings of
which, hanging from a collar, had formed a cloak reaching to
the waist and bordered below with a broad band of tubular
beads of lapis, carnelian, and gold; against the right arm were
three long gold pins with lapis heads and three amulets in the
form of fish, two of gold and one of lapis, and a fourth in the
form of two seated gazelles, also of gold.

The head-dress, whose remains covered the crushed skull,
was a more elaborate edition of that worn by the court ladies;
its basis was a broad gold ribbon festooned in loops round the
hair—and the measurement of the curves showed that this
was not the natural hair but a wig padded out to an almost
grotesque size; over this came three wreaths, the lowest hanging down over the forehead, of plain gold ring pendants, the
second of beech leaves, the third of long willow leaves in sets
of three with gold flowers whose petals were of blue and white
inlay; all these were strung on triple chains of lapis and
carnelian beads. Fixed into the back of the hair was a golden
'Spanish comb' with five points ending in lapis-centred gold
flowers. Heavy spiral rings of gold wire were twisted into the
side curls of the wig, huge lunate ear-rings of gold hung down
to the shoulders, and apparently from the hair also hung on
each side a string of large square stone beads with, at the end
of each, a lapis amulet, one shaped as a seated bull and the
other as a calf. Complicated as the head-dress was, its different
parts lay in such good order that it was possible to reconstruct
the whole and exhibit the likeness of the queen with all her
original finery in place.

For the purposes of exhibition a plaster cast was made from
a well-preserved female skull of the period (the queen's own
skull was too fragmentary to be used), and over this my wife
modelled the features in wax, making this as thin as possible
so as not to obliterate the bone structure; the face was passed
by Sir Arthur Keith, who has made a special study of the Ur
and all 'Ubaid' skulls, as reproducing faithfully the character
of the early Sumerians [Fig. 16]. On this head was put a wig of
the correct dimensions dressed in the fashion illustrated by terracotta figures which, though later in date, probably represent
an old tradition. The gold hair-ribbon had been lifted from
the tomb without disturbing the arrangement of the strands,
these having been first fixed in position by strips of glued paper
threaded in and out between them and by wires twisted round

the gold; when the wig was fitted on the head, the hair-ribbon was balanced on the top and the wires and paper bands were cut, and the ribbon fell naturally into place and required no further arranging. The wreaths were re-strung and tied on in the order noted at the time of excavation. Though the face is not an actual portrait of the queen, it gives at least the type to which she must have conformed, and the whole reconstructed head presents us with the most accurate picture we are likely ever to possess of what she looked like in her lifetime.

By the side of the body lay a second head-dress of a novel sort. On to a diadem, made apparently of a strip of soft white leather, had been sewn thousands of minute lapis lazuli beads, and against this background of solid blue was set a row of exquisitely fashioned gold animals, stags, gazelles, bulls, and goats, with between them clusters of pomegranates, three fruits hanging together shielded by their leaves, and branches of some other tree with golden stems and fruit or pods of gold and carnelian, while gold rosettes were sewn on at intervals, and from the lower border of the diadem hung palmettes of twisted gold wire.

The bodies of two women attendants were crouched against the bier, one at its head and one at its foot, and all about the chamber lay strewn offerings of all sorts, another gold bowl, vessels of silver and copper, stone bowls, and clay jars for food, the head of a cow in silver, two silver tables for offerings, silver lamps, and a number of large cockle-shells containing green paint; such shells are nearly always found in women's graves, and the paint in them, presumably used as a cosmetic, may be white, black, or red, but the normal colour is green. Queen Shub-ad's shells were abnormally big, and with them were found two pairs of imitation shells, one in silver and one in gold, each with its green paint.

The discovery was now complete and our earlier difficulty was explained: King A-bar-gi's grave and Queen Shub-ad's were exactly alike, but whereas the former was all on one plane, the queen's tomb-chamber had been sunk below the general level of her grave-pit. Probably they were husband and wife: the king had died first and been buried, and it had been the queen's wish to lie as close to him as might be; for this end the grave-diggers had reopened the king's shaft, going down in it until the top of the chamber vault appeared; then they had stopped work in the main shaft but had dug down

at the back of the chamber a pit in which the queen's stone
tomb could be built. But the treasures known to lie in the
king's grave were too great a temptation for the workmen;
the outer pit where the bodies of the court ladies lay was
protected by six feet of earth which they could not disturb
without being detected, but the richer plunder in the royal
chamber itself was separated from them only by the bricks of
the vault; they broke through the arch, carried off their spoil,
and placed the great clothes-chest of the queen over the hole
to hide their sacrilege.

No other explanation than this would account for the
plundered vault, lying immediately below the unplundered
grave of the queen. And on this showing we have two almost
identical burials, the sole difference being that in the queen's
case the tomb-chamber is below the level at which the other
victims lie, and for this too the sentimental motive is sufficient.
What the two graves tell us is quite clear so far as it goes.

To begin with, a more or less rectangular shaft was dug
down into the mixed soil of the rubbish-mounds to a depth of
some thirty feet; at the top the shaft might measure as much
as forty-five feet by thirty; the earth walls were necessarily
sloped but were kept as nearly vertical as might be, and on
one side there was cut an entrance in the form of a steeply
sloped or stepped passage running down from ground level.
On the bottom of the shaft, but occupying only a small part
of its area, the tomb-chamber was built, with stone walls and
brick vaulted roof and a door in one of the longer sides. The
royal body was carried down the sloping passage and laid in
the chamber, sometimes, perhaps generally, inside a wooden
coffin, though Queen Shub-ad lay upon an open wooden bier
and another queen in the only other undisturbed burial was
apparently stretched upon the floor of the tomb. Three or four
of the personal attendants of the dead had their place with
him or her in the tomb-chamber; thus, two were crouched by
Shub-ad's bier and one lay a little apart and four shared the
tomb of the other (nameless) queen; in the plundered tombs
scattered bones betrayed the presence of more than one body.
These attendants must have been killed, or drugged into
insensibility, before the door of the tomb-chamber was walled
up. The owner of the tomb was decked with all the finery
befitting his station and with him in the chamber were set all
such objects as we find in the graves of commoners, the only

difference being that they are more numerous and of more precious material—the vessels for food and drink may be of gold and silver instead of clay—the attendants, on the other hand, while they wear what we may call their court dresses, are not laid out properly as for burial but are in the attitudes of those who serve, and they are unprovided with any grave equipment of their own; they are part of the tomb furniture.

When the door had been blocked with stone and brick and smoothly plastered over, the first phase of the burial ceremony was complete. The second phase, as best illustrated by the tombs of Shub-ad and her husband, was more dramatic. Down into the open pit, with its mat-covered floor and mat-lined walls, empty and unfurnished, there comes a procession of people, the members of the dead ruler's court, soldiers, men-servants and women, the latter in all their finery of brightly-coloured garments and head-dresses of carnelian and lapis lazuli, silver and gold, officers with the insignia of their rank, musicians bearing harps or lyres, and then, driven or backed down the slope, the chariots drawn by oxen or by asses, the drivers in the cars, the grooms holding the heads of the draught-animals, and all to take up their allotted places at the bottom of the shaft and finally a guard of soldiers forms up at the entrance. Each man and woman brought a little cup of clay or stone or metal, the only equipment needed for the rite that was to follow. There would seem to have been some kind of service down there, at least it is certain that the musicians played up to the last; then each of them drank from their cups a potion which they had brought with them or found prepared for them on the spot—in one case we found in the middle of the pit a great copper pot into which they could have dipped—and then lay down and composed themselves for death. Some-body came down and killed the animals (we found their bones on the top of those of the grooms, so they must have died later) and perhaps saw to it that all was decently in order—thus, in the king's grave the lyres had been placed on the top of the bodies of the women players, leant against the tomb wall—and when that was done earth was flung in from above, over the unconscious victims, and the filling-in of the grave-shaft was begun.

SIR AUSTEN LAYARD

THE WINGED LIONS OF NIMRUD

(From NINEVEH AND BABYLON. *John Murray*, 1853)

A little over one hundred years ago Austen Layard, un-hampered by any archæological tradition, was burrowing about in the ruins of the ancient cities of Assyria. The record he left of his pioneer work is most vivid—not only was he discovering the treasures contained in the Assyrian mounds but he was working with Arab tribesmen who still lived and fought with all the gusto of their age-old customs.

In the following extract Layard tells how he brought two of the huge human-headed animals from the Palace at Nimrud back to England. These two great lions guarded the entrance to one of the principal apartments of the palace of Ashur-nasir-pal II. In 879 B.C., the fifth year of the King's reign, the building was completed, and to celebrate the opening a banquet was given to 69,574 persons. This we know from an historic sandstone monument discovered recently by Professor M. E. L. Mallowan who was leading an expedition sent out by the British School of Archæology in Iraq. The powerful city of Nimrud—Calah of the Old Testament—was burnt and sacked some time between 614 and 612 B.C., probably by a combined army of the Baby-lonians and the Medes as they fought their victorious way along the Tigris. They set fire to the palace, stripped the buildings of their roofs, and it was not long before the tops of the walls fell in and buried the great monuments beneath them.

Some of the treasures, including the human-headed lions that Layard retrieved, may be seen in the British Museum today.

THE gigantic human-headed lions, first discovered in the north-west palace at Nimrud, were still standing in their original position. Having been carefully covered up with earth previous to my departure in 1848, they had been pre-served from exposure to the effects of the weather, and to wanton injury on the part of the Arabs. The Trustees of the British Museum wishing to add these fine sculptures to the national collection, I was directed to remove them entire. A road through the ruins, for their transport to the edge of the mound, was in the first place necessary, and it was commenced early in December. They would thus be ready for embarkation as soon as the waters of the river were sufficiently high to bear a raft so heavily laden, over the rapids and shallows between Nimrud and Baghdad. This road was dug to the level of the pavement or artificial platform, and was not finished till the end of February, as a large mass of earth and rubbish had to be taken away to the depth of fifteen or twenty feet. . . .

By 28th January, the colossal lions forming the portal to the great hall in the north-west palace of Nimrud were ready to be dragged to the river-bank. The walls and their sculptured panelling had been removed from both sides of them, and they stood isolated in the midst of the ruins. We rode one calm cloudless night to the mound, to look on them for the last time before they were taken from their old resting-places. The moon was at her full, and as we drew nigh to the edge of the deep wall of earth rising around them, her soft light was creeping over the stern features of the human heads, and driving before it the dark shadows which still clothed the lion forms. One by one the limbs of the gigantic sphinxes emerged from the gloom, until the monsters were unveiled before us. I shall never forget that night, or the emotions which those venerable figures caused within me. A few hours more and they were to stand no longer where they had stood unscathed amidst the wreck of man and his works for ages. It seemed almost sacrilege to tear them from their old haunts to make them a mere wonder-stock to the busy crowd of a new world. They were better suited to the desolation around them; for they had guarded the palace in its glory, and it was for them to watch over it in its ruin. Sheikh Abd-ur-Rahman, who had ridden with us to the mound, was troubled with no such reflections. He gazed listlessly at the grim images, wondered at the folly of the Franks, thought the night cold, and turned his mare towards his tents. We scarcely heeded his going, but stood speechless in the deserted portal until the shadows again began to creep over its hoary guardians.

Beyond the ruined palaces a scene scarcely less solemn awaited us. I had sent a party of Jebours to the bitumen springs, outside the walls to the east of the enclosure. The Arabs, having lighted a small fire with brushwood, awaited our coming to throw the burning sticks upon the pitchy pools.

A thick heavy smoke, such as rose from the jar on the seashore when the fisherman had broken the seal of Solomon, rolled upwards in curling volumes, hiding the light of the moon, and spreading wide over the sky. Tongues of flame and jets of gas, driven from the burning pit, shot through the murky canopy. As the fire brightened, a thousand fantastic forms of light played amidst the smoke. To break the cindered crust, and to bring fresh slime to the surface, the Arabs threw large stones into the springs; a new volume of fire then burst forth, throwing a deep red glare upon the figures and upon the landscape. The Jebours danced round the burning pools, like demons in some midnight orgy, shouting their war-cry, and brandishing their glittering arms. In an hour the bitumen was exhausted for the time, the dense smoke gradually died away, and the pale light of the moon again shone over the black slime pits.

The colossal lions were moved by still simpler and ruder means than those adopted on my first expedition. They were tilted over upon loose earth heaped behind them, their too rapid descent being checked by a hawser, which was afterwards replaced by props of wood and stone. They were then lowered, by levers and jackscrews, upon the cart brought under them. A road paved with flat stones had been made to the edge of the mound, and the sculpture was, without difficulty, dragged from the trenches.

Beneath the lions, embedded in earth and bitumen, were a few bones, which, on exposure to the air, fell to dust before I could ascertain whether they were human or not. The sculptures rested simply upon the platform of sun-dried bricks without any other sub-structure, a mere layer of bitumen, about an inch thick, having been placed under the plinth.

Owing to recent heavy rains, which had left in many places deep swamps, we experienced much difficulty in dragging the cart over the plain to the riverside. Three days were spent in transporting each lion. The men of Naifa and Nimrud again came to our help, and the Abou-Salman horsemen, with Sheikh Abd-ur-Rahman at their head, encouraged us by their presence. The unwieldy mass was propelled from behind by enormous levers of poplar wood; and in the costumes of those who worked, as well as in the means adopted to move the colossal sculptures, except that we used a wheeled cart instead of a sledge, the procession closely resembled that which in days of yore transported the same great figures, and which we see so graphically represented on the walls of Kouyunjik. As they had been brought so were they taken away.

It was necessary to humour and excite the Arabs to induce them to persevere in the arduous work of dragging the cart through the deep soft soil into which it continually sank. At one time, after many vain efforts to move the buried wheels, it was unanimously declared that Mr. Cooper, the artist, brought ill luck, and no one would work until he retired. The cumbrous machine crept onwards for a few more yards, but again all exertions were fruitless. Then the Frank lady would bring good fortune if she sat on the sculpture. The wheels rolled heavily along, but were soon clogged once more in the yielding soil. An evil eye surely lurked among the workmen or the bystanders. Search was quickly made, and one having been detected upon whom this curse had alighted, he was ignominiously driven away with shouts and execrations. This impediment having been removed, the cart drew nearer to the village, but soon again came to a standstill. All the Sheikhs were now summarily degraded from their rank and honours, and a weak ragged boy having been dressed up in tawdry kerchiefs, and invested with a cloak, was pronounced by Hormuzd to be the only fit chief for such puny men. The cart moved forwards, until the ropes gave way, under the new excitement caused by this reflection upon the character of the Arabs. When that had subsided, and the presence of the youthful Sheikh no longer encouraged his subjects, he was as summarily deposed as he had been elected, and a greybeard of ninety was raised to the dignity in his stead. He had his turn; then the most unpopular of the Sheikhs were compelled to lie down on the ground, that the groaning wheels might pass over them, like the car of Juggernaut over its votaries. With yells, shrieks, and wild antics the cart was drawn within a few inches of the prostrate men. As a last resource I seized a rope myself, and with shouts of defiance between the different tribes, who were divided into separate parties and pulled against each other, and amidst the deafening *tahlel* of the women, the lion was at length fairly brought to the water's edge.

The winter rains had not yet swelled the waters of the river so as to enable a raft bearing a very heavy cargo to float with safety to Baghdad. It was not until the month of April, after I had left Mosul on my journey to the Khabour, that the floods,

from the melting of the snows in the higher mountains of
Kurdistan, swept down the valley of the Tigris. I was consequently obliged to confide the task of embarking the sculptures to Behnan, my principal overseer, a Mosuleean stone-
cutter of considerable skill and experience, Mr. Vice-consul
Rassam kindly undertaking to superintend the operation.
Owing to extraordinary storms in the hills, the river rose
suddenly and with unexampled rapidity. Mr. and Mrs. Rassam
were at the time at Nimrud, and the raftsmen had prepared
the rafts to receive the lions. It was with difficulty that they
escaped before the flood, from my house in the village to the
top of the ruins. The Jaif was one vast sea, and a furious wind
drove the waves against the foot of the mound. The Arabs had
never seen a similar inundation, and before they could escape
to the high land many persons were overwhelmed in the
waters.

When the flood had subsided, the lions on the river bank,
though covered with mud and silt, were found uninjured.
They were speedily placed on the rafts prepared for them, but
unfortunately during the operation one of them, which had
previously been cracked nearly across, separated into two
parts. Both sculptures were doomed to misfortune. Some
person, uncovering the other during the night, broke the nose.
I was unable to discover the author of this wanton mischief.
He was probably a stranger, who had some feud with the
Arabs working in the excavations.*

The rafts reached Baghdad in safety. After receiving the
necessary repairs they floated onwards to Busrah. The waters
of the Tigris throughout its course had risen far above their
usual level. The embankments, long neglected by the Turkish
government, had given way, and the river, bursting from its
bed, spread itself over the surrounding country in vast lakes
and marshes. One of the rafts was dragged into a vortex which
swept through a sluice newly opened in the crumbling bank.
Notwithstanding the exertions of the raftsmen, aided by the
crew of a boat that accompanied them, it was carried far into
the interior, and left in the middle of a swamp, about a mile
from the stream. The other raft fortunately escaped, and
reached Baghdad without accident.

For some time the stranded raft was given up for lost.

* Both sculptures have, however, been completely restored in the British
Museum.

Fortunately it bore the broken lion, or its recovery had probably been impossible. Captain Jones, with his usual skill and intrepidity, took his steamer over the ruined embankment, and into the unexplored morass. After great exertion, under a burning sun in the midst of summer, he succeeded in placing the two parts of the sculpture on large boats provided for the purpose, and in conveying them to their destination.*

* These accidents, and even still more the carelessness afterwards shown in bringing them to this country, have much injured these fine specimens of Assyrian sculpture, which now stand in a great hall of the British Museum.

PERSIA

SIR HENRY RAWLINSON

BEHISTUN: A KEY TO HISTORY

(From NOTES ON SOME PAPER CASTS OF CUNEIFORM INSCRIPTIONS UPON THE SCULPTURED ROCK AT BEHISTUN. *Society of Antiquaries of London*, 1852)

The Empire of the Persians was greater than the world had ever seen before. It stretched from the River Indus to the Ægean, from the Indian Ocean to the deserts of the Caspian, and from 521-485 B.C. it was ruled by Darius the Great, a humane and intelligent dictator.

He caused a triumphal monument to be carved high up on the rock at Behistun, five hundred feet above the highway which runs from Babylon to the Iranian plateau. The men of the caravans could see the monument and knew Darius to be the Great King. There, high above them, was a picture of him receiving homage, and on great prepared spaces in the rock the powerful edict was written in three languages. 'I am Darius the Great King, the King of Kings . . .' and so on. It was written in Old Persian, Elamite and Babylonian, and in each case the wedge-shaped script known as cuneiform was used. Cuneiform—it was a script that had baffled the archæologists. Many tablets and inscriptions from Babylonia and Assyria were in their hands but they were unable to read the story. Colonel Henry Rawlinson, between the years 1835 and 1847, made the perilous ascent to the inscriptions and took exact copies of the texts, and from his knowledge of Pehlevi he was able eventually to solve the Old Persian inscription because the two languages belong to the same family. Having deciphered the Old Persian it was possible to solve the Babylonian and finally to deal with the Elamite, the most difficult language, which presents many problems to this day.

The importance of Colonel Rawlinson's work is that he provided the key to the understanding of all Asiatic languages written in cuneiform—and the following is the script of an address he gave to the Society of Antiquaries in which he describes how it was he was able to make the copies of the texts on the Behistun rock.

THE rock or, as it is usually called by the Arab geographers, the mountain of Behistun, is not an isolated hill, as has been sometimes imagined. It is merely the terminal point of a long, narrow range which bounds the plain of Kermanshah to the eastward. This range is rocky and abrupt throughout, but at the extremity it rises in height, and becomes a sheer precipice. The altitude I found by careful triangulation to be 3,807 feet, and the height above the plain at which occur the tablets of Darius is perhaps 500 feet, or something more.

Notwithstanding that a French antiquarian commission in Persia described it a few years back to be impossible to copy the Behistun inscriptions, I certainly do not consider it any great feat in climbing to ascend to the spot where the inscriptions occur. When I was living at Kermanshah fifteen years ago, and was somewhat more active than I am at present, I used frequently to scale the rock three or four times a day without the aid of a rope or ladder; without any assistance, in fact, whatever. During my late visits I have found it more convenient to ascend and descend by the help of ropes where the track lies up a precipitate cleft, and to throw a plank over those chasms where a false step in leaping across would probably be fatal. On reaching the recess which contains the Persian text of the record, ladders are indispensable in order to examine the upper portion of the tablet; and even with ladders there is considerable risk, for the foot-ledge is so narrow, about eighteen inches or at most two feet in breadth, that with a ladder long enough to reach the sculptures sufficient slope cannot be given to enable a person to ascend, and, if the ladder be shortened in order to increase the slope, the upper inscription can only be copied by standing on the topmost step of the ladder, with no other support than steadying the body against the rock with the left arm, while the left hand holds the note-book, and the right hand is employed with the pencil. In this position I copied all the upper inscriptions, and the interest of the occupation entirely did away with any sense of danger.

To reach the recess which contains the Scythic [Elamite] translation of the record of Darius is a matter of far greater difficulty. On the left-hand side of the recess alone is there any foot-ledge whatever; on the right-hand, where the recess, which is thrown a few feet further back, joins the Persian tablet, the face of the rock presents a sheer precipice, and it is necessary therefore to bridge this intervening space between the left-hand of the Persian tablet and the foot-ledge on the left-hand of the recess. With ladders of sufficient length, a bridge of this sort can be constructed without difficulty; but my first attempt to cross the chasm was unfortunate, and might have been fatal, for, having previously shortened my only ladder in order to obtain a slope for copying the Persian upper legends, I found, when I came to lay it across to the recess in order to get at the Scythic translation, that it was not sufficiently long to lie flat on the foot-ledge beyond. One side of the ladder would alone reach the nearest point of the ledge, and, as it would of course have tilted over if a person had attempted to cross in that position, I changed it from a horizontal to a vertical direction, the upper side resting firmly on the rock at its two ends, and the lower hanging over the precipice, and I prepared to cross, walking on the lower side, and holding to the upper side with my hands. If the ladder had been a compact article, this mode of crossing, although far from comfortable, would have been at any rate practicable; but the Persians merely fit in the bars of their ladders without pretending to clench them outside, and I had hardly accordingly begun to cross over when the vertical pressure forced the bars out of their sockets, and the lower and unsupported side of the ladder thus parted company from the upper, and went crashing down over the precipice. Hanging on to the upper side, which still remained firm in its place, and assisted by my friends, who were anxiously watching the trial, I regained the Persian recess, and did not again attempt to cross until I had made a bridge of comparative stability. Ultimately I took the casts of the Scythic writing by laying one long ladder, in the first instance, horizontally across the chasm, and by then placing another ladder, which rested on the bridge, perpendicularly against the rock.

The Babylonian transcript at Behistun is still more difficult to reach than either the Scythic or the Persian tablets. The writing can be copied by the aid of a good telescope from below, but I long despaired of obtaining a cast of the inscription; for I found it quite beyond my powers of climbing to reach the spot where it was engraved, and the cragsmen of the place, who were accustomed to track the mountain goats over the entire face of the mountain, declared the particular block inscribed with the Babylonian legend to be unapproachable. At length, however, a wild Kurdish boy, who had come from a distance, volunteered to make the attempt, and I promised him a considerable reward if he succeeded. The mass of rock in question is scarped, and it projects some feet over the Scythic recess, so that it cannot be approached by any of the ordinary means of climbing. The boy's first move was to squeeze himself up a cleft in the rock a short distance to the left of the projecting mass. When he had ascended some distance above it, he drove a wooden peg firmly into the cleft, fastened a rope to this, and then endeavoured to swing himself across to another cleft at some distance on the other side; but in this he failed, owing to the projection of the rock. It then only remained for him to cross over to the cleft by hanging on with his toes and fingers to the slight inequalities on the bare face of the precipice, and in this he succeeded, passing over a distance of twenty feet of almost smooth perpendicular rock in a manner which to a looker-on appeared quite miraculous. When he had reached the second cleft the real difficulties were over. He had brought a rope with him attached to the first peg, and now, driving in a second, he was enabled to swing himself right over the projecting mass of rock. Here, with a short ladder, he formed a swinging seat, like a painter's cradle, and, fixed upon this seat, he took under my direction the paper cast of the Babylonian translation of the records of Darius which is now at the Royal Asiatic Society's rooms, and which is almost of equal value for the interpretation of the Assyrian inscriptions as was the Greek translation on the Rosetta Stone for the intelligence of the hieroglyphic texts of Egypt. I must add, too, that it is of the more importance that this invaluable Babylonian key should have been thus recovered, as the mass of rock on which the inscription is engraved bore every appearance, when I last visited the spot, of being doomed to a speedy destruction, water trickling from above having almost separated the overhanging mass from the rest of the rock, and its own enormous weight thus threatening very shortly to bring it thundering down into the plain, dashed into a thousand fragments.

The method of forming these paper casts is exceedingly simple, nothing more being required than to take a number of sheets of paper without size, spread them on the rock, moisten them, and then beat them into the crevices with a stout brush, adding as many layers of paper as it may be wished to give consistency to the cast. The paper is left there to dry, and on being taken off it exhibits a perfect reversed impression of the writing.

FRANCE

GLYN DANIEL

LASCAUX: A PAINTED CAVE

(From LASCAUX AND CARNAC. *Lutterworth Press*, 1955)

The great Ice Age came to an end about 20,000 B.C. and our hard-pressed early ancestors eked out a frugal existence in meagre rock shelters. They were entirely dependent upon their hunting and food-gathering, and the long, cold winters must have been a trial to their courageous spirits. The vegetation was sparse, and terrifying wild beasts such as mammoth and bison roved freely. The challenge to existence was such that these Stone Age men sought an aid from magic, and in the dark caves naturally formed in the limestone cliffs near their shelters they painted scenes which might magically help them with their hunting.

There are many of these cave paintings and in the following extract Dr. Glyn Daniel records the most recent series found at Lascaux on the Vézère in France.

THE story of the discovery of Lascaux has often been told; indeed, like the '*Toros! Toros!*' story about Altamira, it is now one of the standard anecdotes of prehistory. Nevertheless, because it is true and relevant and exciting, it demands re-telling. On the morning of 12th September, 1940, when the Battle of Britain was being fought out and France itself was divided into an occupied and a so-called unoccupied zone by a line that ran from Bordeaux north-east to Burgundy, five young men from Montignac went out rabbit-shooting. They were Ravidat, Marsal, Queroy, Coencas and Estreguil. Ravidat, Marsal and Queroy were local boys; the other two were refugees from occupied France. Ravidat, aged seventeen at the time, was the oldest of the five and the leader of the party. They had with them two guns and a dog—a famous dog to whom archæologists should erect a statue—the little dog Robot.

The boys climbed about on the ridge of hill called Lascaux, which belonged, and still belongs, to the Comtesse de la Rochefoucauld, and which lies to the south of Montignac. Twenty years before their expedition a storm had blown down a tall fir tree, and the hole revealed by its torn roots did not fill in. A donkey fell in, broke his legs and died. On 12th September, 1940, the dog Robot disappeared down this hole. The young lads had no idea what had happened to him and shouted his name. Muffled barks came from within the hillside, and at last they stood around the tree-root hole where the donkey's bones lay whitening. Ravidat, the dog's owner, decided he would go down the pot-hole and rescue Robot. The five young men widened the hole with sticks and knives until it was large enough for Ravidat to slip through. He slithered down and fell on to the slippery floor of a cave twenty-five feet below the surface of the earth. The other lads followed him. They lit matches. There was Robot, and in the gloom around them on the walls of the cave were the magnificent paintings of the main hall of Lascaux which now make the small town of Montignac a place of world pilgrimage— horses, stags, bulls. Marsal, Ravidat and the others were the first to see this art for fifteen thousand years.

When they got back to Montignac, the five lads did not at first tell anyone else. For five days they kept their amazing discovery to themselves, and while they guarded this secret they explored the cave fully. Then they told their old schoolmaster, Léon Laval, who had taught them about Upper Palæolithic art and taken them to see the famous caves of Font de Gaume and Combarelles. Monsieur Laval thought they were pulling his leg, but changed his mind as soon as he got inside the cave. On 21st September the Abbé Breuil, who was staying at Brive, on the borders of occupied and unoccupied France, twenty miles from Lascaux, came over to see the new discoveries. He studied the paintings and drawings together with other prehistorians. Less than a year later the Abbé Breuil, Monsieur Peyrony and the Comte Begouen held a sort of informal inquest on their discoveries and decided that Lascaux was to be closed to the general public for the time being. In October 1940, a preliminary report by Breuil was presented to the *Académie des Inscriptions et des Belles Lettres* in Paris. In this report Breuil said that if Altamira was to be described as the capital of prehistoric cave art, then Lascaux was the '*Versailles de la Préhistoire*'.

After the war the Historical Monuments Commission of the French Government took charge of Lascaux. The *aménagements* are, as always—or almost always—in French antiquities, very well carried out indeed. Two massive doors protect the cave from the outside, and the cave itself is well and tastefully lit. Lascaux is just over a mile from the centre of Montignac, and is open to the public most of the year from 9.30 a.m. to 12 noon and, after a long midday gap, from 2 p.m. to 7 p.m. Two of the guides and guardians are the original discoverers, Ravidat and Marsal, although, alas! the real original discoverer, the little dog Robot, is no longer.

I first saw Lascaux in the spring of 1948 soon after it had been opened to the public, and have seen it almost every year since then. It is one of the prehistoric sites which never palls and which always, on revisiting, lives up to one's memory. Indeed, it always seems to me that the Lascaux in one's mind's eye is not so brightly coloured and the painting not so vigorous and breath-taking as the reality when one sees it again. A visit to Lascaux is not long; unlike Font de Gaume and Combarelles, there is no scrabbling through narrow passages and a long walk before the Palæolithic art is found. You pass through the second door, and within a minute from leaving the sunshine of the hillside, and the postcard stalls, you are in the main hall, or, as it is often called, the Hall of Bulls. This is a good name, because one of the main features of this first hall is the fresco of bulls. Four of these bulls are intact, and there are two others not complete—the largest of the bulls is as much as sixteen to seventeen feet long. They are all painted in black outline, probably with manganese, and the surfaces spotted with black. These fine black bulls are painted on top of older paintings in dark red ochre.

The first animal on the left as you enter the hall, and before you see the bulls, has caused a great deal of comment, and has been nicknamed the Unicorn. Its body is that of a rhinoceros, but its head (according to Miss Dorothea Bate) is that of the Pantholops, the Tibetan antelope. From the main Hall of the Bulls a passage leads off to the right, and another goes straight on. For convenience of reference we may call these the right-hand passage, leading to apse and nave, and the left-hand gallery; these are the names by which they are known in the books. The right-hand passage or lateral passage, as it is sometimes called, leads into two wider areas of the cave called the apse and the nave; among the astonishing treasures of Palæolithic art to be found here are the frieze of stags' heads, and the splendid pair of male bison, tail to tail, painted in dark brown. On the left-hand wall of the nave below the forelegs of a painted cow are curious polychrome, nine-squared, chequered figures. No one has succeeded in explaining the meaning of these figures, unless they be, like one explanation of the 'tectiforms', marks of artists or tribes.

From the end of the apse there opens up a vertical pit or well, which is not open to the general public. At the bottom is painted one of the most remarkable things in the art of Lascaux, or, for that matter, in Upper Palæolithic art. This scene is reproduced here because of the impracticability of visiting it [Fig. 18]. First of all there is a bison with head down; he has been transfixed with a spear and his innards are tumbling out. In front of the bison is a very oddly drawn man falling backwards. The man has a birdlike head. Near by is a bird on the end of a rod, and in front a spear-thrower, while further to the left is a rhinoceros. What does all this mean? Has the hunter himself been killed in the act of hunting the bison, and is the bird on a stick his totem? It is all a matter of guesswork. We have already commented on the absence of human beings from Palæolithic art, and the absence of scenes. That is what makes the Lascaux painting so unusual and interesting.

The left-hand or axial gallery has many wonderful works of Upper Palæolithic art; the visitor should note particularly the frieze of little horses over which a cow seems to be jumping [Fig. 17], the horse falling upside down at the end of the gallery, and the roof paintings of cattle and horses. You can visit Lascaux many times and still be surprised by the delightful masterpieces you had forgotten about. The best way to get the most out of Lascaux is to visit it in the morning, having driven over from Les Eyzies. Then, with the paintings and engravings fresh in your mind, climb up the hill to the little farmhouse which now advertises itself as the Café-Restaurant Bellevue. Here you can sit on the terrace looking out over the Vézère Valley, or, best of all, eat lunch. You will be given an inexpensive and exciting lunch—*foie gras, confit d'oie, omelette aux truffes, salade,* and then perhaps *beignets,* with white and red wine—everything, including the wine, but with the exception of the salt and sugar, the product of this charming hill farm.

And while you savour your lunch you can think over the problems which crowd into the average traveller's mind as he sees Lascaux. Is it genuine? We have spoken about the controversy relating to the authenticity of Upper Palæolithic art that raged from the discoveries at Altamira to the famous day

at La Mouthe. By now most people accept Upper Palæolithic
cave art, but when Lascaux was discovered, some said, could
it be true? It was and is so much fresher and better than the
other sites. That is due to the special circumstances of its
position. It is well below the level of the ground and unaffected
by frosts and changes of temperature. Many of the paintings,
moreover, have been made on a thin calcitic film, which acted
as a varnish on the wall and has made the paintings keep their
colour more than have those of many other Palæolithic caves.
Yes, Lascaux is a genuine example of Upper Palæolithic cave
art. What, then, do these painted and engraved caves mean?

The entrance by which you now visit Lascaux is not the
original entrance. This has yet to be found, and it may well
be that, originally, at Lascaux, as at Font de Gaume and
Combarelles and La Mouthe, a long passage led in from the
open hillside to the dark, painted chambers within the hill.
Why were these caves so painted with animals? Many explanations have been suggested at various times. These are not houses
or tombs. They must be special places of assembly, not, surely,
art galleries, but of special assembly for magico-religious
purposes. Did you notice at Lascaux that some of the animals
have arrows and spears drawn across their sides? This is quite
a common feature of Upper Palæolithic art, and the most
cogent explanation we can give at present is that perhaps
sympathetic magic was practised in these dark caves; that
around and on the paintings and drawings rites were enacted
that guaranteed or were hoped to guarantee, the success of the
hunter. This is, of course, guesswork, as all explanations of
prehistoric art and symbolism must be, but it seems to fit all
the puzzling features of this art: its remoteness, the fact that
paintings and drawings are often put on top of each other, the
concentration of animals—and often of pregnant animals—
and the arrows and spears drawn in the sides. These were
probably fertility and hunting magics, and in other Palæolithic
sites, though not in these we have been looking at in the
Dordogne, there are clearly shown masked human figures.
These masked figures—humans wandering around in animal
masks—were the priests or medicine men, or artists as well,
who controlled and assisted at whatever rites took place in
these ritual caves.

But even if we do not agree with this explanation of the
purpose of this art, we can admire its vigour and energy and

natural charm. We have to wait a great time in the history of
European art before we find again the same naturalistic
treatment of animals we have here. Indeed, some would say
that there is a Walt Disney feel about some of the animals—
like the little horses in the axial gallery. Your lunch finished,
go down the hill and see Lascaux again, and pause, taking in
these fine bulls and horses. You are seeing these paintings
under the best possible circumstances of lighting. We know
that prehistoric man, who fifteen to twenty thousand years
ago explored these caves and made these paintings, had lamps
of limestone in which he burnt vegetable oil, but it would be
a very different thing from our present viewing when the great
Hall of the Bulls was full of masked figures lit up by these
guttering lamps and by torches. It may well be that we in the
present century are the first persons to see Upper Palæolithic
art well lit as art, and not as magical symbolism.

Two final reflections as you drive down in your car or walk
down to Montignac. Are the paintings at Lascaux fading, due
to their present exposure to light and their inspection every day
by hundreds of visitors? There is a persistent legend that this
is so, but I am assured by Monsieur Blanc of Les Eyzies, who
is Supervisor of Antiquities in the Dordogne, that it is a legend,
and that no change in the appearance and quality of these
paintings has taken place since that day in September 1940,
when the five boys burst into the hillside and dropped into
this prehistoric temple. And, finally, how many more such
exciting stories are there to be told in the next fifty to a hundred
years? It is only fifteen years since Lascaux was discovered.
I cannot believe that the quiet Dordogne hillsides do not
contain more prehistoric sanctuaries. But it may well take more
than the accident of a dog falling down a hole to find them.

SIBERIA

BASSETT DIGBY

THE FROZEN MAMMOTH

(From THE MAMMOTH. *Witherby*, 1926)

For thousands of years Stone Age man shared the forests **and** rivers of Northern Europe and Siberia with great beasts that are now extinct: beasts such as the woolly rhinoceros, sabre-toothed tiger, great stag, cave bear, and mammoth. Terrifying as these animals must have appeared to our prehistoric ancestors, we find that man with his wits, flint weapons, and his magic conquered them and in the end survived, whereas they died out about 1500 years ago.

For our knowledge of mammoths, we do not have to rely only on the portraits drawn by primitive man on the cave walls at Les Eyzies; some have survived in the flesh, until our own times, preserved in the northern ice. These intact specimens come from Siberia and from them we learn that the great beasts ate grasses, pine tips, and buttercups, since these plants have been collected, frozen, from their stomachs. We know, too, that they stood twelve to thirteen feet high at the shoulder, that their tusks could be as much as nine to ten feet in length and that their huge hides were covered with a rusty brown hair.

The following is an extract in which Mr. Bassett Digby quotes the diary of Dr. Hertz, who dug one of these formidable prehistoric animals from the ground.

IN the winter of 1900 a Cossack named Yavlovski, living at Sredne-Kolymsk, a small Arctic settlement of stockaded log cottages in north-east Siberia, obtained by barter a number of mammoth tusks which had been collected, here and there, along the shores of rivers in the wilderness by a Lamut tribesman.

'You see that one,' said the Lamut, pointing to a fine tusk on the heap. 'I chopped that one out of the mouth of one of those great hairy devils, up on the undercliff of the Beresovka.'

'Really?' said Yavlovski, dissimulating his excitement and proceeding to pump the Lamut, whose name was Tarabykin, for further information, then bidding him keep his mouth shut.

'There ought to be money in this,' rightly concluded Yavovski. Not knowing enough of the world, however, to know

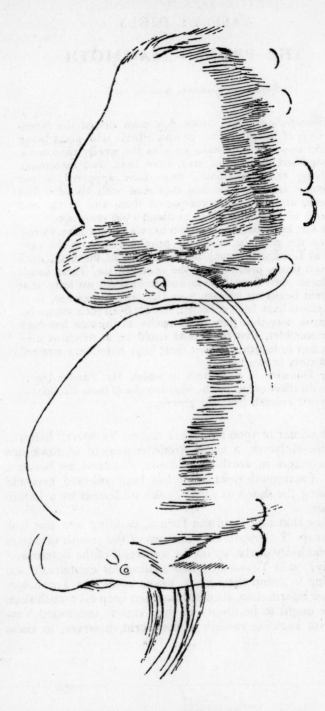

Two mammoths drawn by Old Stone Age man on the walls of the cave at Font-de-Gaume (*After* Breuil)

how to set about capitalizing his knowledge, he sought the advice of one of the Russian police officials—Sredne-Kolymsk was a place of exile for political exiles—and this man, whose name was Horn, lent his aid in return for a share of the proceeds.

Horn sent a message through to Governor-General Skripitsin at Yakutsk, and he telegraphed to Petrograd. Thus it was that in the middle of April, 1901, the Imperial Academy of Sciences in the capital received tidings of a mammoth, apparently in a satisfactory state of preservation, frozen into the cliff of the River Beresovka, a right tributary of the River Kolyma, 200 miles north-east of Sredne-Kolymsk, and 800 miles west of Behring Strait.

A grant of £1,630 for the recovery of the carcass was promptly made by Count Witte, the Finance Minister. An expedition was fitted out under the leadership of Dr. Otto F. Hertz, a zoologist on the staff of the Academy's museum. He was accompanied by M. E. V. Pfizenmeyer, a zoological preparator of the same institution, and M. D. P. Sevastianov, a geological expert of Yurievsk University.

The expedition left Petrograd on 4th May. The story of how it found and excavated the great prehistoric monster of flesh and blood, which had been lying in cold storage for perhaps half-a-million years, is best told by Dr. Hertz's own diary, jotted down from day to day.

13th September-18th September

Upon reaching Mysova, on the Kolyma river, I was informed that the Cossack, Yavlovski, had gone but a few days previously to the region where the mammoth had been found, about eighty-five miles away, having understood that the Academy expedition would not reach Sredne-Kolymsk before winter. I was told that upon his return, in three or four days, I should be able to continue the journey.

Yavlovski arrived on 16th September, and though the tidings he brought were somewhat discouraging, there was still hope for success. He had intended to visit the mammoth region in the spring, but had been hindered by a serious illness from which he had only recently recovered. Were it not for this mishap he would have covered the find with stones and earth, and thus prevented it from injury by rain and beasts of prey.

K

He tells us that rains during the summer had washed a mass of earth down the slope in which the mammoth lies, so that bones were torn from the hind part of the body, the entire back was exposed, and most of the head skin was devoured by bears and wolves. The trunk had already gone when the carcass was first found. Yavlovski reported that he had collected all the bones lying about, placed them on top of the animal, and covered them with earth and stones, so that no more damage would be likely to result before my arrival. As he saw no hair or wool on the exposed parts, he thought that either there had been none, or else that it had been washed away by the rains.

I am very sorry I could not see the Lamut, S. Tarabykin, who discovered the mammoth, but he was absent at this time. I can, therefore, give the details of the discovery only as related to me, as follows, by Yavlovski:

About the end of August 1900, while the Lamut, Tarabykin, was chasing a deer, he found a mammoth's tusk, weighing about 166 lb., a little above the present find, and, continuing the search, soon discovered the well-preserved head of a mammoth protruding from the ground. On this head, however, there was but one tusk. On account of the superstitious fear that the Lamuts have of whole mammoth bodies, the excavation of which they believe produces sickness, Tarabykin returned to his shelter, about fifteen miles distant, and told of his discovery to the two Lamuts, M. Tapchin and V. Dietkov. These two men visited me twice at the place of discovery and, after close questioning, informed me that at the time of finding the animal the skin upon its head had already partly decayed, and that there was no trunk, or 'nose', as they described it. The Lamuts said that at the part where they chopped off the tusk, on the day following the discovery, there was left only a small piece of decayed skin. They believed that the head had been exposed for about a year before they found it, but insisted that they had never seen it before, as it was the first time they had visited the place, and that they had never previously seen a mammoth. The Lamut, Tapchin, was more than ninety years old.

Toward the middle of September 1900, all three Lamuts went to the Kolyma, where they sold the tusks to Yavlovski, telling him that the smaller tusk, weighing a little over 63 lb., belonged to a mammoth which was probably still in the ground in a good state of preservation, but which they dared not touch. The Cossack, Yavlovski, being more intelligent, understood the importance of this discovery, and agreed to meet them on 14th November and go with them to see the mammoth. He told the Lamuts that if what they related were true he would report to the Tsar, which might result in the fitting out of an expedition to transport the entire animal to St. Petersburg. This satisfied the Lamuts, but it is to be regretted that Yavlovski did not instruct them to cover the mammoth with earth.

Toward the end of October 1900, Yavlovski, accompanied by the Lamuts, visited the mammoth. He cut a piece of skin from the head, a similar piece from the left thigh, and secured a small portion of the stomach, with its contents, and brought these, together with the tusk, to Sredne-Kolymsk as proofs of the discovery. He gave them to the assistant police commissioner, N. L. Horn, who decided to convince himself of the importance of the find, and then to report the matter to the Governor of Yakutsk. The parts mentioned were forwarded to the Imperial Academy of Sciences at St. Petersburg, where they were due after our departure.

At the end of December, Horn and Yavlovski together examined the mammoth and reported the matter to the Governor of Yakutsk, who sent Horn's report to St. Petersburg.

24th September, 1901

It was so warm today that the soil became loose and easily handled, and I was able to begin the work of excavation.

The mammoth lies a third of a mile from our tents and 115 ft. above the present level of the water, on the left bank of the River Beresovka. The body lies in a cliff that faces east and extends in a semicircle for a mile. . . .

According to the Lamut natives of the region, the head of the mammoth was exposed two years ago by the breaking away of a considerable mass of earth. The rest of the body was exposed only in mid-September 1900. . . .

I began to open up the mammoth mound. The skull was soon exposed. Unfortunately most of the head skin had been devoured by carnivorous animals during the past summer.

To my great surprise I found well-preserved food fragments between the teeth, which proves that our mammoth, after a short death struggle, died in this very position. The fact that what we found was food, and not substance carried into the mouth recently, was later proved by comparing it with the stomach contents.

Upon the left half of the bone between the jaws I could see marks of the axe which the Lamuts used in chopping off the tusk. I could thus determine definitely that the tusk which I had seen in Sredne-Kolymsk was from this particular mammoth, for I had carefully measured and studied the cuts upon it. The right tusk evidently had fallen out long ago, for I could find no traces of its forced severage from the head. The lower jaw, which was fast in the ground, lay upon a large piece of skin which appeared, from subsequent examination, to belong to the upper part of the chest.

I first gave orders carefully to remove the mound of earth about the mammoth, beginning with the soil which had been placed over the head. At a depth of 2 ft. 3 in., we found the left fore-leg, still covered with hair on all sides up to the humerus. The epidermis had apparently completely rotted, but on account of the moist earth the hair still clung to the skin. We may perhaps succeed in getting it, frozen, to St. Petersburg.

So far as a preliminary examination can determine, the hair on the upper part of the fore-leg consists of a yellowish brown matted under-coat, 10-12 in. long, with a thick upper bristle-like coat, the hairs of which have ragged ends, are rust-brown, and from 4-5 in. long. The left fore-leg is bent, so that it is evident that the mammoth tried to crawl out of the pit or crevasse into which probably he fell, but he appears to have been so badly injured by the fall that he could not free himself.

Further excavation exposed the right fore-leg, which had become turned almost horizontally under the abdomen by the beast's fall. Only a very insignificant portion of the upper bristly coat was preserved upon this leg, though the yellowish brown under-coat was preserved in several places. Upon the left hind-leg I also found portions of decayed flesh, in which the muscular bundles were easily discernible. The stench emitted by this extremity was unbearable. We had to stop work every minute or two. A thorough washing failed to remove the horrible smell from our hands, yet we were obliged to perform part of our task with bare hands.

25th September

After we removed the earth from under the left leg, the thick hair on the underside came to view, especially that on the foot joint. Some of the hair fell off with the earth, but the larger part will be saved by bandages. In the midst of the yellowish brown under wool, which resembles in colour the summer coat of a young camel, there are very thickly set hairs of the bristly coat, 4-5 in. long. The colour of this hair on the underside of the leg is roan, while that on the outer and inner side, up to the middle of the fore-leg, is dark brown—somewhat lighter at the ends. Five hoof-shaped blunt nails could also be seen at the end of the digits.

The wool of the left hind-leg, varying in colour from rust-brown to roan, was not so thick as upon the fore-leg, judging by the loosened remains of the hair, and the yellowish brown under-coat was here a little shorter. The length of the ragged end-hairs varies from $1\frac{1}{2}$-5 in. The roots of the hair had rotted away, along with the epidermis.

In the afternoon we dug away the mound of earth to a depth of 8 ft. on the right side of the mammoth. In the mound, lying between the upper layer of earth and the vertical ice-wall, we found roots and other parts of trees and boulders. Beneath this layer of soil, 8 ft. thick, I first struck ice, 7 in. thick; then a thin layer of earth; then another layer of ice, after which the right fore-leg of the mammoth came into view. The wool that had probably covered the upper side of this leg had entirely gone. Most likely it had been torn away by the sliding masses of ice and soil. The same was true of the wool on the other side of the animal.

The right fore-leg was so placed as to indicate that the mammoth, after falling, had supported himself on this leg while trying to step forward with the left one. We concluded that while in this standing position he became exhausted and died on this very spot, and that he had by no means been washed there by the water from elsewhere. The presence of a thick wool shows that the animal was well adapted to endure cold, and it is improbable that he died from hunger, for a large quantity of fragments of food was in his stomach. His head faces south.

26th September

I searched the vicinity for bones of other animals, and found horns of the northern deer lying about everywhere.

27th September

Hoping to find remains of the trunk, I ordered that the mound be opened up further south and south-eastward; but

I made no discovery. This part was no doubt exposed before the rest, and had long ago either decayed or been devoured. I examined every shovelful of earth, but I found only indefinite fragments of very brittle hair.

After dinner I began clearing the ice away from the right side. Near the outside of the right fore-leg the ice was brownish, with bubbles. It was 9 in. thick and 10½ in. over the sole of the right fore-foot, which also faced the south, as did the left hind-leg. Beneath both legs there was a layer of ice 1½ in. thick which, after the final loosening of the animal, was found to extend beneath the whole body. From the right leg northward, in the direction of the high land, the ice ran thicker, being at first 21 in.; while 33½ in. from the foot it was 28½ in. thick. Then came the earth layer. The ice layer, 27¾ in. at its thickest part, extended to the middle of the right side of the abdomen, where it became 4 in. thick.

A very interesting discovery was made at a distance of 5 in. from the upper edge of the sole of the right hind-foot—the very hairy end of the tail, which was thawed out and examined.

28th September

The snow has completely melted from the cliff. I have stopped further excavation, however, until my companions, who were left behind, arrive, and M. Sevastianov can make the geological survey. In order to be able to dismember the mammoth after severe cold weather has set in, I am inclined to build over the carcass a shed that can be heated. I must give orders, one day soon, for the timber to be cut and trimmed. Meanwhile, I have covered it with tarpaulin to protect it from being buried by a sudden heavy snowfall.

29th September

In clear weather I climbed to the top of the hill east of here and collected some fine specimens of mountain flora.

30th September

The cliff region extends along the loop made by the Beresovka and along the deep channel of this river half a mile farther south, where it gradually becomes lower. While the flood waters come down in spring, masses of soil are broken away from the cliff.

Further geological research will determine how the region was formed. Yet, though I am not a geologist, I regard it my duty to express my personal views on the matter. In my opinion, the entire cliff region rests upon a glacier, which was disintegrating and in which there were deep crevasses. The whole was later covered with a layer of soil, upon which doubtless there developed a rich flora that served as excellent food for mammoths and other animals. Whether this flora was identical with the present flora can be determined only when the food fragments found in the mouth and stomach of the mammoth have been examined and compared with the plants I collected on the cliff. The upper layer of earth at that time was not yet firm enough everywhere to support the weight of mammoths. Probably our specimen fell through into a crevasse, which would account for his position and for the fracture of such heavy bones as the pelvis and the right fore-leg. After falling, the mammoth no doubt tried to crawl out, the position of both fore-legs being peculiarly like that of an animal making such an effort, but the injuries were so serious that his strength failed, and he soon perished. . . .

1st October

We moved today from the tents into the new winter house that I have had built in the forest, in a spot sheltered from the north wind. By evening we had settled in nicely, and felt it very comfortable to sit down to supper in a well-warmed room.

2nd October

In several pits in the earth I found well-preserved parts of *Betula nana* (birch), which is absent from exposed places, though in sheltered spots one occasionally finds stems about as thick as a man's arm. The timber with which a shed will be put over the mammoth is already cut and trimmed. We can begin to put it up as soon as our fellow-travellers arrive. Although the mammoth is frozen it smells abominably.

3rd October

M. Pfizenmeyer arrived this afternoon with the rest of the transport equipment. To my surprise, M. Sevastianov was not with him, as he returned from Mysova to Sredne-Kolymsk with M. Horn.

4th October

Today, in our winter quarters, we began to thaw out the end of the tail which we found on the 26th. We soon had to stop, as all the hair threatened to fall off. This piece of tail is 8½ in. long, and the hairs at the end, penetrating an icy earth mass, are 4 in. long. The hairs stand in clusters round the tip of the tail. When warmed, however, these separate from the skin, together with the epidermis. Only at the very end part is the hair still fast in the skin. The hairs on the basal end of the tail and a little farther down are dirty yellow-ochre, and those at the distal end are black. The thin ends of the hair are partly broken off. The hairs at the middle of the tail end are a very few centimetres longer than the others, and their colour is ochre at the base; then black; and at the tip whitish.

The shed over the mammoth is nearly finished. As we proposed to build this structure below the upper wall of the skull, we removed the latter. We were then able to take out the remnants of food from between the molars on the left side. These remnants appear masticated and apparently contain not parts of pine or larch needles, but only bits of various grasses. The imprint of the tooth crenations is well preserved upon the half-chewed food. There is also a small quantity of food upon the well-preserved tongue, but I can secure this only when the lower jaw is removed.

The most devoted mother could not carry her child more carefully than I carried these fragments of antediluvial fauna to our winter hut. When the Lamuts discovered the mammoth they could not see the fragments of food, for the lower jaw was then still in the ground. This was confirmed by Tarabykin's companions, whom I questioned closely on this point.

9th October

Today I took the chief measurements of the mammoth. I also collected the plants which are partly under the snow.

11th October

We have finished the roof over the mammoth.

13th October

We made today the first experiments in heating the shed. The arrangements seem to be excellent. However, we have yet to build a wooden partition, so that the animal may not be exposed directly to the fire, however low it may be. Still it is necessary to keep a steady fire going, day and night, to prevent it freezing again.

14*th October*

As we found the shed too dark for our work, a second opening has been made, near the door. We have put sheets of ice in both openings as windows, and hung an elk's pelt over the doorway.

15*th October*

We have begun to clear away the soil from the occiput and back. In doing so we exposed several broken ribs; we dug up, too, some lumbar vertebrae which had been torn out by wild beasts or else forced out by the sliding earth.

Under the right middle part of the abdomen, which was still covered with soil, we found a yellowish brown under wool, $7\frac{4}{5}$-$11\frac{7}{16}$ in. long. It was so mixed up with mud that we saved only a small portion of it.

We also collected and deposited in a bag the under wool and bristles from the right cheek. The latter are $7\frac{4}{5}$ in. long, and broken off at the ends. The colour varies from black to pale blonde. The black hairs predominate and are lighter toward the ends.

16*th October*

After removing the last layer of earth from the back, some food in the stomach was exposed. It was badly decayed. We could not continue our work on account of the solidly frozen condition of everything. After dinner we removed the right side of the abdomen in order to thaw the interior of the body.

17*th October*

Before noon we removed the left shoulder-blade and part of the ribs. Then we cleaned part of the stomach, which contained an immense quantity of remnants of food. The walls of the stomach first exposed were dark coffee-brown, almost black, and were badly decayed and torn.

We amputated the left front-leg, between the shoulder and fore-leg, this afternoon, in hopes of saving the wool which still clung to the leg and which might have fallen away during subsequent thawing. The amputation was necessitated also by the left side of the abdomen.

18*th October*

We skinned the left side and exposed several ribs, which were mostly very well preserved. The stomach with its contents is becoming more and more exposed, while the other organs are destroyed. Then we skinned the head, of which the following parts were preserved: the cheeks, the right eyelid with the deep eyelash-fold, part of the skin from the sinciput, three-quarters of the upper lip, and the very well-preserved underlip. This latter was also beset by scattered spines or bristles, which, however, adhered to the ground and were mixed up with other hair, so that it was impossible to pick them out. The skin from the head, which was already decayed in several places, we immediately treated with alum and salt.

In the afternoon we removed the left shoulder, leaving on it the tendon and muscular fibres.

The flesh from under the shoulder, fibrous and marbled with fat, is dark red and looks as fresh as well-frozen beef or horse-meat. It looked so appetizing that we wondered for some time whether we would not taste it. But no one would venture to take it into his mouth, and horseflesh was given the preference.

The dogs ate whatever mammoth meat we threw them.

The layer of fat beneath the skin is nine centimetres thick. It is white, odourless, spongy, and readily cut. The flesh between the ribs and skin, as well as the membrane under the ribs, could easily be pulled off in separate layers without special effort.

The skin on the left shoulder is $\frac{741}{1000}$ in. thick, and on the right side $\frac{741}{1000}$ in.

The big clusters of hair that lay in the frozen ground near the lower lip, and which belonged to the chin and chest, are 14 in. long, torn as they are. Estimating the broken-off ends to be one-third the entire length—based on the thickness of the hair at the break—it may be assumed that these hairs were about $19\frac{1}{2}$ in. long. The bristly hairs which stuck in the ground immediately behind the lower lip are black; those pointing toward the fore-legs are ash-blonde. As it is impossible to pick out these hairs uninjured, I shall take the entire clod of earth and keep it frozen.

Of length similar to that of the above-mentioned hairs is the hair shed from the outer side of the left shoulder-blade, which I removed. Judging by the remnants of the separate hard bristle-like hairs which I noticed on the skin, they were of the same length, extending perhaps along the back. Beginning with the destroyed epidermis, up to the very ends, these hairs are ashy or pale blonde. The shoulder bore the longest hair ound thus far, and is probably what has been erroneously called the mammoth 'mane'. The applicability of this term will be possible only when it is proved that no other parts of the mammoth were covered with such long hair.

The hairs upon the belly are reddish brown at the base, chestnut-blonde in the middle, and yellowish at the ends.

The hairs on the left cheek are 9 in. long, partly chestnut-brown to black, partly blonde. The under wool is not so thick as on the other parts of the skin, the hairs being yellowish, as everywhere else, and 13½ in. long. The bristle-like hairs of the spine retain their elasticity so long as they remain in the cold air, but in the warmer temperature of our house they hardened instantly and became very brittle. I keep everything, accordingly, in the natural outdoor temperature.

19th October

We bandaged the left fore-leg, packed it in hay, then wrapped it in sackcloth, so the wool will probably remain intact. In Sredne-Kolymsk we shall sew all these things up in hides, of which I have not enough here.

We have removed from the stomach about 27 lb. more of the remains of food. We then amputated the right fore-leg above the shoulder-blade, cut it open down to the fore-arm, and removed the shoulder-blade, which was broken in the middle, evidently injured when the mammoth fell. We should have liked to transport the leg intact, but it was too heavy for one dog-sledge. The flesh and fat are well preserved, and will be packed for shipment. No hair was found on the outer and anterior sides of the right fore-leg, and from the underside of this leg I succeeded in saving only what I found in beautiful layers of ice.

I collected bits of frozen blood. They looked like small pieces of potassium permanganate. When melted these bits turn into dirty, dark red spots, which are easily washed off. They feel like coarse dry sand. Similar blood occurs also between the stomach and the sternum, whereas blood that was taken from above the sternum and the shoulder-blades had a bright clay-yellow colour and felt like chalk. I placed these two kinds of blood in a bag, separated by a layer of cotton.

The stench is not nearly so bad as it was, perhaps because we have grown accustomed to it.

20th October

After packing the right leg today, we went on cleaning out the stomach. The parts of the stomach that were exposed to the air for any length of time tear even when most carefully touched, just as the membrane beneath the ribs did.

By afternoon we managed to expose the part of the body which we had not yet been able to reach, and which still lay in the frozen soil. This part was $3\frac{1}{2}$ in. lower than the left fore-leg, and 5 in. lower than the sole of the left foot. It proved to be the protruded male genital, $33\frac{1}{2}$ in. long above, and 41 in. long below, four inches above the urinary meatus. The diameter of the flattened-out penis is $7\frac{2}{5}$ in.

21st October

The more the hind-quarters are freed the more difficult the work grows. The left side of the broken pelvis was removed. The flesh beneath the pelvis is still frozen as hard as stone, like the flesh about the shoulder-blades. Near the stomach there is a lump of ice which we must remove little by little. The cross-bone or sacrum was intact.

22nd October

We cut off the left hind-leg this morning, and the right hind one this afternoon. The thigh bones, which were very trouble-some to sever, on account of the frozen meat that surrounds them, were so strongly connected with the tibia that it was necessary to cut all these bones out together, to be dismembered tomorrow.

The colour of the hair of the right hind-femur varies from rust-brown to black. The best preserved of all the hair was that in the fold of the skin between the penis and the left hind-leg. The crumpled hair of the under wool is $11\frac{7}{10}$ to $13\frac{13}{20}$ in. long. The bristly hair is $12\frac{1}{2}$ in. long. I extracted some pathological growths from the right shoulder, and some layers of hair, with careful notes of their position on the body.

23rd October

After removing some 270 lb. of flesh, we started the raising of the abdominal skin, which proved to be still quite bulky. We decided it would have to be cut up. After raising the piece of skin, which weighed about 470 lb., we discovered, to our joy, the entire tail of the mammoth. The joy that possessed us at this new find was so great that, lowering the skin to the ground again, we gave three loud cheers. We could not decide to cut up the still intact piece of skin, as we wanted to be able to take back this interesting object intact to the Academy.

The tail is short, and appears to consist of from twenty-two to twenty-five caudal vertebrae. It is not as long as the drawing made under von Brandt's supervision, and more nearly resembles the tail drawn by Boltunov, though it is defective in other respects.

The hard, bristly hairs, which are broken off to about one-third their length, indicate that the end of the tail was covered with long hairs that became stuck in the layer of ice underneath the entire body. However, these hairs were pulled out of the ice with great care. They are $7\frac{4}{5}$ to $9\frac{3}{4}$ in. long, and, like the bristly hair on the anterior side of the left fore-leg, rusty brown, their somewhat darker colour being due to deterioration under the influence of damp. Some of the hairs are half a millimetre in diameter at the base of the tail. On the underside of the tail they stood closer at the very end. The length of the tail, measured on the underside, is only 14 in., its circumference at the base being $12\frac{1}{2}$ in.

The width of the anal opening is 11 in., and the length of the somewhat drawn-out skin extending between the base of the points and that of the tail is 4 ft. The base of the tail, together with the anus, were located 4 ft. 4 in. lower than the underside of the left hind-tibia.

The reason that Boltunov in his drawing figured excrescences on the fetlocks, which indicated the presence of rudimentary metacarpal and metatarsal bones, is explained by the fact that the mammoth he saw in all probability had just such a mass of hair at the bend of the leg as this mammoth found on the Beresovka.

24th October

Snow fell today. Very soon we shall have to get away. The problem is: which track is the more convenient—down the Beresovka to the Kolyma, or direct overland through the forest? I sent Yavlovski on ahead to examine the forest track.

25th-27th October

We are working unceasingly to get everything ready for our departure, which has been fixed for the 28th. We have prepared ten sledges, each laden with pieces of mammoth. When Yavlovski returned today (the 27th) with tidings that the track through the forest was feasible we were highly delighted.

28th October

As our horses were not enough to take away the whole expedition at once, I sent Yavlovski ahead with parts of the mammoth and some of the men.

7th November

We all met again at Mysova yesterday. As the transport seems to be going ahead smoothly, we went on in advance to Sredne-Kolymsk, where we arrived today.

The expedition then safely accomplished the long sledge journey overland to Yakutsk, up the frozen River Lena, and again overland to Irkutsk. Here, at last, it reached the Trans-Siberian Railway, by which it covered the last lap of its journey to Petrograd.

De Windt, who, with De Clinchamp and Harding, was travelling north down the Lena, on his plucky trek to the Behring Strait, met the party between Olekminsk and Yakutsk. The mammoth had now made itself more at ease, and was travelling on twenty sledges instead of the ten in which it left the Beresovka, records De Windt, who adds that Dr. Hertz had had a difficult journey, the passes being choked with snowdrifts and deer being scarce.

DENMARK

DENMARK

P. V. GLOB

THE MYSTERY OF TOLLUND MAN

(From *Illustrated London News*. 24th November, 1951)

Two thousand years ago a man was hanged at Tollund in
Denmark and his body was thrown into a marsh pool. There
it was preserved intact until 1950.

Professor P. V. Glob of Aarhus University in Denmark
writes of this remarkable find.

PEAT-CUTTING in the Danish bogs frequently brings
objects to light which have lain hidden since before the
written history of the country began. Many of the
treasures of Danish antiquity, such as the 'lurs', the widely-
known Bronze Age trumpets, and many ornaments of gold,
silver and bronze, were found by this process, all of them
objects which would hardly have found their way by chance
into the peat-bogs, but must rather have been deposited there
as offerings to some divine power. A similar interpretation
must be made in the case of the twenty or so ploughs, dating
to the middle of the first millennium B.C., and again of the
human bodies, about forty in all, dating from before the introduction of Christianity, all found in the peat-bogs. Almost
all these objects are characteristically found in quite small
'saucer' bogs, or in small branches of the larger fen areas.

One of the best preserved and most thoroughly investigated
bodies was brought to light in May 1950, in the course of peat-
cutting in Tollund Bog in Central Jutland. While lecturing at
Aarhus University, I received a telephone call from the police,
who informed me of the discovery of a well-preserved corpse
and requested me to investigate the matter, as they suspected
an unsolved murder. A visit to the finding-place, however, a
little elongated peat-bog surrounded by high, steep hills in a
desolate heather-clad area, established that the crime, if crime
it was, had taken place perhaps 2,000 years ago. It was an
amazing sight to see this prehistoric man, his face so well
preserved and as expressive as though he had but a moment
ago fallen asleep. He lay in a contracted position as though
sleeping, with wrinkled brow, closed eyes and mouth fast shut,

with all the appearance of a strong personality [Fig. 19]. Only the dark, brown-leather colour showed his age. But this man of a bygone age had not of his own free will laid himself to sleep on this spot and been covered in the course of centuries by successive layers of peat. A rope formed of two smooth plaited leather thongs lay in a noose round his neck, pulled tight and choking, with the long, free end lying along his back. And he was naked. On his head he bore a skin cap, sewn together from eight pieces of leather with the fur inwards, and fitted with a chin-strap. But the only body clothing was a leather belt knotted in a noose over the stomach. It is obvious that this man, clothed only in cap and belt, had been hanged and then deposited in the bog. But why? It is improbable that a common criminal would have been treated in this way, while many people would regard the fine lines of the Tollund man's countenance as telling against such a theory.

About a hundred bodies of men, women and children have, in the course of the last two centuries, been recovered from peat-bogs in the area covering Jutland, north-west Germany and Holland. Of these only a few can have come there accidentally, drowned in the treacherous bogs, while the lack of burial furnishings shows that there can be no question of normal burial. A characteristic of the majority of the bodies discovered is their scanty attire. Many, like the Tollund man, are practically naked, and many have only a leather cape over their shoulders. Very many have a noose of rope or leather round their necks, while others have crushed heads, broken limbs, or mortal wounds in their body. Some are bound hand and foot, and others are pinned down in the bogs by a wooden stake or a hook, this last being a precaution against haunting. A medieval tradition in this connection relates that King Abel could not, on account of a fratricide, rest in his grave in Schleswig Cathedral, and was therefore exhumed and laid in a near-by bog, held fast by a stake through the body. Ancient writings tell how criminals ended their days staked down in peat-bogs; Tacitus, for example, describing this as a custom of the Germani about A.D. 100, while other early authors tell us that human sacrifices were offered to the gods in Scandinavia right up to the introduction of Christianity about A.D. 1000. Hanging was, moreover, in ancient times not considered a dishonourable death, this viewpoint only coming in with Christianity, based on the fact that hanged men were sacred to Odin, the wise, one-eyed god, one of the chief gods of the close of the heathen period.

There is perhaps reason to emphasize two points in connection with the Tollund man; that he was hanged and that he was naked. Many of the other bodies from the peat bogs are naked, and many still have the rope with which they were hanged around their necks. *And the general belief is that such naked hangings were ritual sacrifices in connection with the great spring fertility festivals of antiquity.* An investigation of the stomach contents of the Tollund man throws an interesting sidelight on the question of the food of prehistoric man. This investigation showed that he had eaten no animal food recently, but only a porridge of vegetables and seeds. This porridge consisted mainly of barley, linseed, 'gold of pleasure' (*Camelina linicola*) and pale persicaria (*Polygonum lapathifolium*), all of which were cultivated during the Iron Age; but, in addition, it contained a number of wild plants such as sheep's sorrel (*Rumex acetosella*), white goosefoot (*Chenopodium album*), brassica, corn spurrey and many others which would scarcely come to be accidentally mixed with the cultivated plants. Thus we may conclude that the seeds of wild plants formed an important part of the diet of prehistoric peoples.

In many ways the Tollund man causes prehistory to live before our eyes. His handsome countenance, fantastically well-preserved, makes a stronger and more real impression than the work of the best sculptor could give. The strange circumstances in which he was found give us a glimpse of a remarkable religion. Well may he have been an offering to the gods to bring fertility and fortune to his fellow-men. The old gods did at least not relinquish him to the scientists of today without exacting their price. They took man for man. While the Tollund man was being lifted from his desolate resting-place to be taken for investigation to the National Museum in Copenhagen, one of the helpers dropped dead, struck down by heart failure. . . .

CHILE

GRETE MOSTNY

THE BOY FROM THE LEAD
MOUNTAIN

(From *Anais do XXXI Congresso Internacional de Americanistas. Sao Paulo* 1955)

Very occasionally startling finds are made which enable us to see, face to face, the people from another country. Such was the discovery of the frozen boy from El Plomo (the Lead) Mountain in Chile in 1954. He came to us from the Inca Empire of the fifteenth century.

In that century the tribe whom we know as the Incas entered upon a meteoric career of conquest and established a rich and wonderful capital at Cuzco in the highlands of Peru. They knitted together their empire with a tremendous system of roads, tunnelling rocks and bridging chasms in the process. For a time they were all-powerful over more than two thousand five hundred miles of South America, from Colombia to Chile, but their greatness fell to Spain in the sixteenth century. The frozen boy in the high mountain was an offering to the Inca gods.

ON 16th February, 1954, two men came to my office in the National Museum of Natural History in Santiago de Chile and told me of an archæological discovery they had made in the mountains. They brought with them a silver statuette dressed in cloth and feathers and described other discoveries, including the 'mummy of a little Indian girl', clothed, according to them, very differently from those in the Museum. With this mummy they found various bags and two toy llamas. I intimated that the Museum would be interested in having this collection, and they told me that the mummy had been found in a tomb at a height of approximately 17,700 feet. As the summer would soon be over, they had thought it wise to keep it at a lower altitude while deciding on its future. So I proposed that they should bring the mummy down to Santiago and report again to the Museum when they had done so. On 15th March, the two men came again with the silver statuette and another made of shell. They informed the Director of the Museum, Don Humberto Fuenzalida, and me that the mummy was in their house at Puente Alto (a village on the outskirts of Santiago). I went to see it next day. The mummy turned out to be the frozen body of a young boy dressed in Inca costume and in such a remarkable state of preservation that he looked as though he were asleep. Realizing the importance of the discovery, I went straight back to the Museum and left a note for the Director urging him to get hold of this collection at once. Consequently Señor Fuenzalida went to Puente Alto the same evening and arranged to buy it for the Museum at a cost of 45,000 Chilean pesos (nearly £100 at that time).

The body was then taken to the Department of Legal Medicine to be kept overnight in their cold-storage room. We thought this would be the best way to treat a frozen body, but after a few hours it became clear that the cold, damp atmosphere could do harm and the doctors decided to keep the body in a dry place at a normal temperature. So the next day we transferred it to the Museum itself where it has remained.

I thought this long introduction necessary, since it is the first official account of this extraordinary discovery. Interest was aroused all over the world and newspapers have published many contradictory reports. . . .

According to the miners who made the discovery, the body was found near the peak of a mountain called 'El Plomo' (meaning the mountain of lead), in the province of Santiago. In this region there are three buildings, called by mountain-climbers the 'Pircas of the Indians'. *Pirca* is a South American word for a dry-stone wall. In one of these, below the level of the ground, was the tomb which contained the boy and his possessions.

A group of mountaineers was near this place on 1st February, 1954, and happened to see two men descending the mountain with a heavy sack on their shoulders. It turned out later that the boy's body was hidden in this sack.

In April, an expedition organized by the National Museum of Natural History and consisting of mountaineers from the Chilean 'Club Andino' under Señor Luis Krahl, together with anthropology students from the university, climbed 'El Plomo' to check the facts given by the miners. Only Señor Krahl and two of his companions reached the place and brought back a report on what they saw.

There are on this mountain two groups of buildings, one at a height of 17,000 feet forming an elliptical enclosure, called by mountaineers the 'altar'. This was probably a Pre-Colombian temple. The major axis of this building deviates twenty-two degrees to the north-east. The second group, at 17,700 feet and very near the peak, consists of three rectangular buildings, the largest with an annexe in one corner. It is worth noting that the major axis deviates twenty-two degrees to the north-east, as in the temple below. The enclosure is just over seven yards long and three and a half yards wide and the walls are about three feet high. The interior is full of earth and stones. In the centre is the tomb, a three-foot cavity, consisting of one floor in a frozen state, covered by a flat stone lid. This report supports the information given by the miners who discovered the body. The miners said that the body was surrounded by its possessions (of funeral furniture), and that it was soft and flexible when they found it and hardened later. In fact, when it arrived at the Museum it was still fairly soft, even though it had been in contact with the air for six weeks.

From Señor Krahl's report, we can deduce that these were ceremonial buildings belonging to a Pre-Colombian race who, from archæological evidence, were the Incas and their contemporaries, though naturally the place may have been frequented by earlier races.

The body was found in a sitting position with the knees doubled up, the legs crossed, the right forearm resting on the knees, the left hand holding the right [Fig. 20]. The last two phalanges (the tips) of the three middle fingers of the left hand showed by their characteristic appearance and colour that they were frozen twenty-four to forty-eight hours before death. It was Senor Krahl who noticed this phenomenon, well known among Andean mountaineers.

Medical and radiological examinations proved that the body was that of a boy; the ossification of his skeleton was not yet complete and he still had some of his first teeth. His age could be ascertained as being between eight or nine years. His first metatarsal (the first bone of the arch of the foot) was unusually short and thick as though reverting to an ancestral type. It was possible to identify such organs as the brain, heart, diaphragm and possibly the liver. On the whole the skeleton was normal though the hands and feet were small in relation to the rest of the body. It was not possible to see any more details by X-ray because of the excessive density of his clothes, accentuated by the partially frozen state of the body and its incipient mummification.

The hair was smooth, greasy and black with the hair follicles well preserved. The face was wide and so was the nose though this was harder to tell because of a post-mortem deformity. But the features could be identified as Mongolian in type, which was to be expected. The colour of the skin varied between different shades of brown, being darker where not protected by clothes. It was possible to make an examination of the blood and conclude that it belonged to group 'O' and to take finger prints which did not differ very much from those observed today.

The boy was dressed in a black woollen tunic, woven in one piece, folded in the middle with a hole for the head which was not quite in the middle of the material. The sides were sewn together and the back and front decorated with a fringe of red wool and four stripes of white vicuña fur. Over his shoulders he wore a woollen rug with a texture like hemp, grey with coloured stripes. This showed signs of hard wear and was darned in several places. It was made of two pieces of cloth sewn together and was tied under his chin with a thick knot which may have caused the post-mortem deformity of the nose, as the head was lying on one side and forwards with the nose resting on the knot. Traces of cloth on the forearms and hands show that the boy had tried to cover these bare parts of his body. He was wearing leather, fur-trimmed moccasins, made in one piece with an embroidered strap, which was sewn onto the leather with a welt. The only seam was in the middle of the toe. The moccasins did not show much sign of wear and the sole was perfectly clean.

. His head-dress consisted of a band from which hung a long thick fringe of black wool. A crest of black and white condor feathers was joined to the centre fastening of this band and placed on the head in such a way that the feathers stayed erect on the forehead. A woollen cord passing under the chin kept the head-dress in place. He also wore the characteristic *Llautu* (head-band worn by the Incas and their subjects). The head was encircled five times with a well-twisted black cord and the turns fastened together by another cord which passed under the chin.

He had a silver ornament shaped like a double crescent with

holes in the top so that it could hang over his chest. When the body was brought to the Museum this ornament had become detached and was found in the folds of the *Llautu*. On his right forearm was a bracelet made of one sheet of silver, trapezoid in form and curved to fit the arm. This was fastened by a thin thread of wool passing through two holes on the inside edge.

His hair reached below his shoulders and was arranged in a great many small fine plaits. His face was painted red with diagonal yellow stripes.

He carried a hanging bag made from a rectangular piece of woven cloth, folded in the middle and sewn up the sides. This contained remnants of cocoa leaves. Apart from his actual clothing, he had with him another bag, made in the same way but entirely covered with red and white feathers. This was packed tightly with cocoa leaves. There were five more bags made of a thin skin which was probably part of the intestine of a mammal of the llama species. The two largest contained little balls of human hair, odds and ends of red wool, and a coarse substance not yet analysed. Another contained nail parings, very irregularly cut, milk teeth, very much worn down, and also a tiny piece of red wool. The other two also contained nail parings and wool.

Also in the collection were two small figures, thought to be llamas or some other animal of that species. One was a male animal made of a gold and silver alloy, the other, carved out of shell, was smaller and less detailed.

Buried separately but in the same enclosure was a figure of a woman standing about four inches high, made in beaten silver and soldered together. The arms were folded with the hands between the breasts, the hair parted in the middle and falling in two plaits over the shoulders. The figure was elaborately dressed in the manner of the Inca women. Five of these clothed figures are known already, three in gold, one silver and one shell. These were also found on 'El Plomo'. Our figure and the one made of shell are the only ones found with a head-dress.

From this discovery various conclusions can be drawn. The body was that of a boy of eight or nine years, a subject of the Incas. But we do not know to which of the many races of the Inca Empire he belonged. His head-dress gives us a clue, since the chroniclers of the time all stress the fact that Indians from different parts of the realm were distinguished by their different head-dresses which they were forbidden to change under the threat of dire punishment. Nobody has yet described a head-dress such as the one worn by this boy. There are, however, some indications that the boy belonged to a people of the Altiplano (the high mountain area of the Andes). It seems that the people of the Altiplano wore moccasins instead of sandals. The chest ornament is identical with one found on the island of Titicaca and with another in a drawing of a chieftain from Collasuyu. This chieftain also wore a bracelet like the boy's and it is known that the rich people of La Paz wore bracelets of gold and silver. The crest of condor feathers is another indication that he came from the Altiplano. In the corner of the drawing of the Collasuyu chieftain a condor is depicted on a shield.

The boy wore a black *Llautu*, one of the privileges conceded by the Inca to a conquered nation—in the ceremonies of *Capac Raymi* the young candidates also wore black *Llautu*. But the boy from 'El Plomo' was too young for this ceremony. On the other hand there were some tribes who always wore the black *Llautu*.

Both tunic and rug were made of rough, ordinary cloth. The tunic was so short that it barely covered the boy's trunk while the general rule was that it should reach the middle of the thigh. But we must not forget that he was a child and we know little of the way children were dressed. We can tell from drawings that his tunic was not identical with that worn by a Royal Prince, but it does seem probable that this boy was the son of a provincial nobleman, or at any rate of a rich man.

The boy was not of an age to wear trousers or to have his ears pierced. According to Inca custom, a youth received his first pair of trousers at the age of fourteen or fifteen at a special ceremony at which all those of noble blood had to pass tests of physical prowess to gain the privilege of pierced ears, trousers, the carrying of arms, and the cutting of their hair. They would then be given their real names too.

In his short life the child from 'El Plomo' would already have passed through one ceremony which would have taken place when he was one or two years old. On this occasion his most senior uncle would cut his hair and his nails and give him the name he would keep until puberty. The hair and nail parings would be kept carefully, and in fact we found them, together with his milk teeth, in the little bags of animal gut.

By the time of his death the boy's hair had grown and reached below his shoulders. It seems to have been arranged for a special occasion just before his death. One of the most interesting features of the 'El Plomo' discovery was the painting of the face. The colour red seems to have been a favourite and was used by warriors to frighten the enemy and also for feasts and dances.

But how did the boy come to be buried on top of the mountain? It is known that the Incas and other Andean races attributed supernatural powers to the mountains. The higher and more imposing the mountain, the greater its power, and they had a special reverence for those covered with eternal snow. 'El Plomo' was one of these, hence the buildings found on or near the peak and the traces of paths leading up to them. The place has long been known by miners and muleteers and they called the buildings, as I have said, the 'Pircas of the Indians'. Many years ago the same miner who discovered the boy's body found gold and silver statues in one of the buildings. But these have long since been sold and nobody has been able to trace their present owners. Mountaineers have said that there is another place among these buildings which may contain the body of yet another sacrificed child. I have no doubt that the body now in the National Museum of Natural History *was* a human sacrifice.

Most of the chroniclers of old Peru agree that human sacrifices existed in the time of the Incas. On special occasions men, women and children were sacrificed as tribute from the provinces of the Empire. These sacrifices were offered when a new Inca came to the throne, in time of victory, when the Inca was ill, or in the case of any calamity. There were four ways of sacrificing the victims: strangulation, pulling out the heart, crushing the neck with a stone, and burying alive. It seems that this last method of sacrificing children was more common among the mountain people. Sometimes they were sacrificed in pairs, a boy and a girl, the children being about ten years old. The victims were dressed in their best clothes. Among the objects that accompanied them to the grave, little figures of llamas in gold and silver have been specially mentioned. Certainly the feather bag containing cocoa leaves was part of this funeral furniture while the hanging bag and the small bags containing wool, nails and teeth were among the personal belongings of the victim.

The boy on 'El Plomo' was certainly buried alive. It has been seen from radiological examination that his body suffered no wound or shock. He would have been given a strong intoxicating beverage called *chicha* to drink and taken to the tomb in an alcoholic stupor and would have been frozen to death before he could recover as we can see from the peaceful expression on his face.

ITALY

AUGUST MAU

POMPEII: A CITY BURIED ALIVE

(From POMPEII: ITS LIFE AND ART. *Macmillan*, 1899)

Towards the end of August in A.D. 79 the town of Pompeii was obliterated.

The following extracts are not archæological reports of discoveries but are accounts of how a whole city was buried and lost, and thereby preserved for the archæologists. Excavations at Pompeii at the foot of Mount Vesuvius on the west coast of Italy have proceeded intermittently through the centuries; but from 1860 onwards a systematic plan has been followed and slowly the town is emerging from the pall of volcanic ash which smothered it nineteen hundred years ago.

August Mau has synthesized the work of many an archæologist and he is able to paint a vivid picture of those fateful days.

At the end of his description I have included two contemporary letters written by the Younger Pliny to Tacitus, which bring home to us the unspeakable horror of the disaster.

PREVIOUS to the terrible eruption of 79, Vesuvius was considered an extinct volcano. 'Above these places,' says Strabo, writing in the time of Augustus, 'lies Vesuvius, the sides of which are well cultivated, even to the summit. This is level, but quite unproductive. It has a cindery appearance; for the rock is porous and of a sooty colour, the appearance suggesting that the whole summit may once have been on fire and have contained craters, the fires of which died out when there was no longer anything left to burn.'

Earthquakes, however, were of common occurrence in Campania. An especially violent shock on 5th February, A.D. 63, gave warning of the reawakening of Vesuvius. Great damage was done throughout the region lying between Naples and Nuceria, but the shock was most severe at Pompeii, a large part of the buildings of the city being thrown down. The prosperous and enterprising inhabitants at once set about rebuilding. When the final catastrophe came, on 24th August, A.D. 79, most of the houses were in a good state of repair, and the rebuilding of at least two temples, those of Apollo and of Isis, had been completed. This renewing of the city, caused by the earthquake, may be looked upon as a fortunate circumstance for our studies [Figs. 21, 22].

Our chief source of information for the events of 24th-26th August, 79, is a couple of letters of the Younger Pliny to Tacitus, who purposed to make use of them in writing his history. Pliny was staying at Misenum with his uncle, the Elder Pliny, who was in command of the Roman fleet. In the first letter he tells of his uncle's fate. On the afternoon of the twenty-fourth, the Admiral Pliny set out with ships to rescue from impending danger the people at the foot of Vesuvius, particularly in the vicinity of Herculaneum. He came too late; it was no longer possible to effect a landing. So he directed his course to Stabiæ, where he spent the night; and there on the following morning he died, suffocated by the fumes that were exhaled from the earth. The second letter gives an account of the writer's own experiences at Misenum.

To this testimony little is added by the narrative of Dion Cassius, which was written a century and a half later and is known to us only in abstract; Dion dwells at greater length on the powerful impression which the terrible convulsion of nature left upon those who were living at that time. With the help of the letters of Pliny, in connection with the facts established by the excavations, it is possible to picture to ourselves the progress of the eruption with a fair degree of clearness.

The subterranean fires of Vesuvius pressed upward to find an outlet. The accumulations of volcanic ash and pumice-stone that had been heaped up on the mountain by former eruptions were again hurled to a great height, and came down upon the surrounding country. On the west side of Vesuvius they mingled with torrents of rain, and flowed as a vast stream of mud down over Herculaneum. On the south side, driven by a north-west wind as they descended from the upper air, they spread out into a thick cloud, which covered Pompeii and the plain of Sarno. Out of this cloud, first broken fragments of pumice-stone—the average size not larger than a walnut—rained down to the depth of eight to ten feet; then followed volcanic ash, wet as it fell by a downpour of water, to the depth of six or seven feet. With the storm of ashes came successive shocks of earthquake.

Such was, in outline, the course of the eruption. It must

have begun early in the morning of the 24th, and the stream of mud must have commenced immediately to move in the direction of Herculaneum; for shortly after one o'clock on that day the Admiral Pliny at Misenum received letters from the region threatened, saying that the danger was imminent, and that escape was possible only by sea. Even then the Younger Pliny saw, high above Vesuvius, the cloud, shaped like an umbrella pine, which was to rain down destruction on Pompeii. Toward evening, the ships off Herculaneum ran into the hail of pumice-stone, which, during the night, reached Stabiæ and so increased in violence that the Admiral Pliny was obliged to leave his sleeping-room from fear that the door would be blocked up by the falling masses.

Early in the morning of the 25th there was a severe shock of earthquake, which was felt as far as Misenum. Then the ashes began to fall, and a cloud of fearful blackness, pierced through and through with flashes of lightning, settled down over land and sea. At Misenum, even, it became dark; 'not,' says Pliny, 'as on a cloudy night when there is no moon, but as in a room which has been completely closed.'

How long the storm of ashes lasted we can only infer from this, but when it ceased the sun had not yet set. In Misenum, which the shower of pumice-stone had not reached, everything was covered with a thick layer of ashes. Although the earthquake shocks continued, the inhabitants went back into their houses. But Pompeii and Stabiæ had been covered so deep that only the roofs of the houses, where these had not fallen in, projected above the surface; and Herculaneum had wholly disappeared.

All the plain of the Sarno was buried, as were also the slopes of the mountains of the south. Stabiæ, as we have seen, lay at the foot of the mountains, on the coast. It had been destroyed by Sulla in the Social War; its inhabitants, forced to scatter, settled in the surrounding country. In the years 1749-82 numerous buildings were excavated in the vicinity, in part luxurious country seats, in part plain farm buildings; but the excavations were afterwards filled up again. The covering of Stabiæ was like that of Pompeii, only not so deep.

Herculaneum was covered with the same materials; they were not, however, deposited in regular strata, but were mixed together, and being drenched with water, hardened into a kind of tufa which in places reached a depth of sixty-five feet.

Excavation at Herculaneum is in consequence extremely difficult; and the difficulty is further increased by the fact that a modern city, Resina, extends over the greater part of the ancient site. The excavations thus far attempted have in most cases been conducted by means of underground passageways. The statement that Herculaneum was overflowed by a stream of lava, though frequently repeated, is erroneous.

The woodwork of buildings in Pompeii has in many cases been preserved, but in a completely charred condition. Frequently where walls were painted with yellow ochre it has turned red, especially when brought immediately into contact with the stratum of ashes—a change which this colour undergoes when it is exposed to heat. Nevertheless, the inference would be unwarranted that the products of the eruption fell upon the city red-hot and caused a general conflagration. The fragments of pumice-stone could scarcely have retained a great degree of heat after having been so long in the air; it is evident from Pliny's narrative that they were not hot.

With the ashes a copious rain must have fallen; for the bodies of those who perished in the storm of ashes left perfect moulds, into a number of which soft plaster of Paris has been poured, making those casts of human figures which lend a melancholy interest to the collections in the little Museum at Pompeii. The extraordinary freshness of these figures, without any suggestion of the wasting away after death, is explicable only on the supposition that the enveloping ashes were damp, and so commenced immediately to harden into a permanent shape. If the ashes had been dry and had packed down and hardened afterwards, we should be able to trace at least the beginnings of decay.

Neither the pumice-stone nor the ashes, then, could have set wood on fire. The woodwork must have become charred gradually from the effect of moisture, as in the case of coal, and the change in the colour of the yellow ochre must be due to some other cause than the presence of heat. This is all the more evident from the fact that vestiges of local conflagrations, confined within narrow limits, can here and there be traced, kindled by the masses of glowing slag which fell at the same time with the pumice-stone, or by the fires left burning in the houses.

From the number of skeletons discovered in the past few decades, since an accurate record has been kept, it has been estimated that in Pompeii itself, about two thousand persons perished. As the city contained a population of twenty thousand or more, it is evident that the majority of the inhabitants fled; since the eruption commenced in the morning, while the hail of pumice-stone did not begin till afternoon, those who appreciated the greatness of the danger had time to escape. It is, however, impossible to say how many fled when it was already too late, and lost their lives outside the city. Mention has already been made of some who perished at the harbour; others who went out earlier to the Sarno may have made good their escape. Of those who remained in the city part were buried in the houses—so with twenty persons whose skeletons were found in the cellar of the villa of Diomedes; others, as the hail of pumice-stone ceased, ventured out into the streets, where they soon succumbed to the shower of ashes that immediately followed. As the bodies wasted away little except the bones was left in the hollows formed by the ashes that hardened around them, and the casts already referred to, which have been made from time to time since 1863, give in some cases a remarkably clear and sharp representation of the victims.

The Emperor Titus sent a commission of senators into Campania to report in what way help could best be rendered. A plan was formed to rebuild the cities that had been destroyed, and the property of those who died without heirs was set aside for this purpose. Nothing came of it, however, so far as our knowledge goes. Pompeii is indeed mentioned in the Peutinger Table, a map for travellers made in the third century, but the name was apparently given to a post station in memory of the former city. Conclusive evidence against the existence of a new city is the absence of any inscriptions referring to it.

LETTERS FROM THE YOUNGER PLINY TO TACITUS
(From PLINY. LETTERS. *Heinemann*, 1915)

Your request that I would send you an account of my uncle's end, so that you may transmit a more exact relation of it to posterity, deserves my acknowledgements; for if his death shall be celebrated by your pen, the glory of it, I am aware, will be rendered for ever deathless. For notwithstanding he perished, as did whole peoples and cities, in the destruction of a most beautiful region, and by a misfortune memorable enough to promise him a kind of immortality; notwithstanding he has himself composed many and lasting works; yet I am persuaded, the mentioning of him in your immortal writings, will greatly contribute to eternize his name. Happy I esteem those whom Providence has gifted with the ability either to do things worthy of being written, or to write in a manner worthy of being read; but most happy they, who are blessed with both talents: in which latter class my uncle will be placed both by his own writings and by yours. The more willingly do I undertake, nay, solicit, the task you set me.

He was at that time with the fleet under his command at Misenum. On the 24th of August, about one in the afternoon, my mother desired him to observe a cloud of very unusual size and appearance. He had sunned himself, then taken a cold bath, and after a leisurely luncheon was engaged in study. He immediately called for his shoes and went up an eminence from whence he might best view this very uncommon appearance. It was not at that distance discernible from what mountain this cloud issued, but it was found afterwards to be Vesuvius. I cannot give you a more exact description of its figure, than by resembling it to that of a pine-tree, for it shot up a great height in the form of a trunk, which extended itself at the top into several branches; because, I imagine, a momentary gust of air blew it aloft, and then failing, forsook it; thus causing the cloud to expand laterally as it dissolved or possibly the downward pressure of its own weight produced this effect. It was at one moment white, at another dark and spotted, as if it had carried up earth or cinders.

My uncle, true savant that he was, deemed the phenomenon important and worth a nearer view. He ordered a light vessel to be got ready, and gave me the liberty, if I thought proper, to attend him. I replied I would rather study; and, as it happened, he had himself given me a theme for composition. As he was coming out of the house he received a note from Rectina, the wife of Bassus, who was in the utmost alarm at the imminent danger (his villa stood just below us, and there was no way to escape but by sea); she earnestly entreated him to save her from such deadly peril. He changed his first design and what he began with a philosophical, he pursued with an heroical turn of mind. He ordered large galleys to be launched, and went himself on board one, with the intention of assisting not only Rectina, but many others; for the villas stand extremely thick upon that beautiful coast. Hastening to the place from whence others were flying, he steered his direct course to the point of danger, and with such freedom from fear, as to be able to make and dictate his observations upon the successive motions and figures of that terrific object.

And now cinders, which grew thicker and hotter the nearer he approached, fell into the ships, then pumice-stones too with stones blackened, scorched and cracked by fire, then the sea ebbed suddenly from under them, while the shore was blocked up by landslips from the mountains. After considering a moment whether he should retreat, he said to the captain who was urging that course, 'Fortune befriends the brave; carry me to Pomponianus.' Pomponianus was then at Stabiæ*, distant by half the width of the bay (for, as you know, the shore, insensibly curving in its sweep, forms here a receptacle for the sea). He had already embarked his baggage; for though at Stabiæ the danger was not yet near, it was full in view, and certain to be extremely near, as soon as it spread; and he resolved to fly as soon as the contrary wind should cease. It was full favourable, however, for carrying my uncle to Pomponianus. He embraces, comforts, and encourages, his alarmed friend, and in order to soothe the other's fears by his own unconcern, desires to be conducted to a bathroom; and after having bathed, he sat down to supper with great cheerfulness, or at least (what is equally heroic) with all the appearance of it.

In the meanwhile Mount Vesuvius was blazing in several places with spreading and towering flames, whose refulgent brightness the darkness of the night set in high relief. But my uncle, in order to soothe apprehensions, kept saying that some fires had been left alight by the terrified country people, and what they saw were only deserted villas on fire in the abandoned district. After this he retired to rest, and it is most certain that his rest was a most genuine slumber; for his breathing, which, as he was pretty fat, was somewhat heavy and sonorous, was heard by those who attended at his chamber-door. But the court which led to his apartment now lay so deep under a mixture of pumice-stones and ashes, that if he had continued longer in his bedroom, egress would have been impossible. On being aroused, he came out, and returned to Pomponianus and the others, who had sat up all night. They consulted together as to whether they should hold out in the house, or

* Now called Castel è Mar di Stabia in the gulf of Naples.

wander about in the open. For the house now tottered under repeated and violent concussions, and seemed to rock to and fro as if torn from its foundations. In the open air, on the other hand, they dreaded the falling pumice-stones, light and porous though they were; yet this, by comparison, seemed the lesser danger of the two, a conclusion which my uncle arrived at by balancing reasons, and the others by balancing fears. They tied pillows upon their heads with napkins; and this was their whole defence against the showers that fell around them.

It was now day everywhere else, but there a deeper darkness prevailed than in the most obscure night; relieved, however, by many torches and divers illuminations. They thought proper to go down upon the shore to observe from close at hand if they could possibly put out to sea, but they found the waves still ran extremely high and contrary. There my uncle having thrown himself down upon a disused sail, repeatedly called for, and drank, a draught of cold water; soon after, flames and a strong smell of sulphur, which was the forerunner of them, dispersed the rest of the company in flight; him they only aroused. He raised himself up with the assistance of two of his slaves, but instantly fell; some unusually gross vapour, as I conjecture, having obstructed his breathing and blocked his windpipe, which was not only naturally weak and constricted, but chronically inflamed. When day dawned again (the third from that he last beheld) his body was found entire and uninjured, and still fully clothed as in life; its posture was that of a sleeping, rather than a dead man.

Meanwhile my mother and I were at Misenum. But this has no connection with history, and your inquiry went no farther than concerning my uncle's death. I will therefore put an end to my letter. Suffer me only to add, that I have faithfully related to you what I was either an eye-witness of myself, or heard at the time, when report speaks most truly. You will select what is most suitable to your purpose; for there is a great difference between a letter, and an history; between writing to a friend and writing for the public. Farewell.

.   .   .

The letter which, in compliance with your request, I wrote to you concerning the death of my uncle, has raised, you say, your curiosity to know not only what terrors, but what

calamities I endured when left behind at Misenum (for there
I broke off my narrative).

'Though my shock'd soul recoils, my tongue shall tell.'

My uncle having set out, I gave the rest of the day to study
—the object which had kept me at home. After which I
bathed, dined, and retired for short and broken slumbers.
There had been for several days before some shocks of earthquake, which the less alarmed us as they are frequent in
Campania; but that night they became so violent that one
might think that the world was not being merely shaken but
turned topsy-turvy. My mother flew to my chamber; I was
just rising, meaning on my part to awaken her, if she was
asleep. We sat down in the forecourt of the house, which
separated it by a short space from the sea. I know not whether
I should call it courage or inexperience—I was not quite
eighteen—but I called for a volume of Livy, and began to read,
and even went on with the extracts I was making from it, as
if nothing were the matter. Lo and behold, a friend of my
uncle's, who was just come to him from Spain, appears on the
scene; observing my mother and me seated, and that I have
actually a book in my hand, he sharply censures her patience
and my indifference; nevertheless I still went on intently with
my author.

It was now six o'clock in the morning, the light still ambiguous and faint. The buildings around us already tottered,
and though we stood upon open ground, yet as the place was
narrow and confined, there was certain and formidable danger
from their collapsing. It was not till then we resolved to quit
the town. The common people follow us in the utmost con-
sternation, preferring the judgement of others to their own
(wherein the extreme of fear resembles prudence), and impel
us onwards by pressing in a crowd upon our rear. Being got
outside the houses we halt in the midst of a most strange and
dreadful scene. The coaches which we had ordered out, though
upon the most level ground, were sliding to and fro, and could
not be kept steady even when stones were put against the
wheels. Then we beheld the sea sucked back, and as it were
repulsed by the convulsive motion of the earth; it is certain at
least the shore was considerably enlarged, and now held many
sea animals captive on the dry sand. On the other side, a

black and dreadful cloud bursting out in gusts of igneous serpentine vapour now and again yawned open to reveal long fantastic flames, resembling flashes of lightning but much larger.

Our Spanish friend already mentioned now spoke with more warmth and instancy: 'If your brother—if your uncle,' said he, 'is yet alive, he wishes you both may be saved; if he has perished, it was his desire that you might survive him. Why therefore do you delay your escape?' We could never think of our own safety, we said, while we were uncertain of his. Without more ado our friend hurried off, and took himself out of danger at the top of his speed.

Soon afterwards, the cloud I have described began to descend upon the earth, and cover the sea. It had already begirt the hidden Capreæ, and blotted from sight the promontory of Misenum. My mother now began to beseech, exhort and command me to escape as best I might; a young man could do it; she, burdened with age and corpulency, would die easy if only she had not caused my death. I replied, I would not be saved without her, and taking her by the hand, I hurried her on. She complies reluctantly and not without reproaching herself for retarding me. Ashes now fall upon us, though as yet in no great quantity. I looked behind me; gross darkness pressed upon our rear, and came rolling over the land after us like a torrent. I proposed while we yet could see, to turn aside, lest we should be knocked down in the road by a crowd that followed us and trampled to death in the dark. We had scarce sat down, when darkness overspread us, not like that of a moonless or cloudy night, but of a room when it is shut up, and the lamp put out. You could hear the shrieks of women and crying children, and the shouts of men; some were seeking their children, others their parents, other their wives or husbands, and only distinguishing them by their voices; one lamenting his own fate, another that of his family; some praying to die, from the very fear of dying; many lifting their hands to the gods; but the greater part imagining that there were no gods left anywhere, and that the last and eternal night was come upon the world.

There were even some who augmented the real perils by imaginary terrors. Newcomers reported that such or such a building at Misenum had collapsed or taken fire—falsely, but they were credited. By degrees it grew lighter; which we imagined to be rather the warning of approaching fire (as in truth it was) than the return of day: however, the fire stayed at a distance from us: then again came darkness, and a heavy shower of ashes; we were obliged every now and then to rise and shake them off, otherwise we should have been buried and even crushed under their weight. I might have boasted that amidst dangers so appalling, not a sigh or expression of fear escaped from me, had not my support been founded in that miserable, though strong consolation, that all mankind were involved in the same calamity, and that I was perishing with the world itself.

At last this dreadful darkness was attenuated by degrees to a kind of cloud or smoke, and passed away; presently the real day returned, and even the sun appeared, though lurid as when an eclipse is in progress. Every object that presented itself to our yet affrighted gaze was changed, cover'd over with a drift of ashes, as with snow. We returned to Misenum, where we refreshed ourselves as well as we could, and passed an anxious night between hope and fear; though indeed with a much larger share of the latter, for the earthquake still continued, and several enthusiastic people were giving a grotesque turn to their own and their neighbours' calamities by terrible predictions. Even then, however, my mother and I, notwithstanding the danger we had passed, and that which still threatened us, had no thoughts of leaving the place, till we should receive some tidings of my uncle.

And now, you will read this narrative, so far beneath the dignity of a history, without any view of transferring it to your own; and indeed you must impute it to your own request, if it shall appear scarce worthy of a letter. Farewell.

SOURCES

The editor and publishers wish to thank the authors, agents and publishers of the various works from which the extracts in *A Book of Archæology* have been taken, for their kindness in allowing this copyright material to be reprinted.

'The World of Meket-Rē' from *Models of Daily Life in Ancient Egypt from the Tombs of Meket-Re' at Thebes* (Vol. XVIII), by H. E. Winlock. Published for the Metropolitan Museum of Art by the Harvard University Press.

'The Discovery of the Dead Sea Scrolls' from *The Dead Sea Scrolls*, by J. M. Allegro. Penguin Books.

'The Treasure Ship of Sutton Hoo' from *Recent Archæological Excavations in Britain* (Ch. VII—'The Excavation of the Sutton Hoo Ship Burial', by C. W. Phillips), edited by R. L. S. Bruce-Mitford. Routledge & Kegan Paul.

'Stonehenge: a Prehistoric Temple' from *Stonehenge*, by R. J. C. Atkinson. Hamish Hamilton.

'Maiden Castle: the First British War Cemetery' from *Maiden Castle, Dorset*, by Sir Mortimer Wheeler. Report of the Research Committee of the Society of Antiquaries of London, No. XIII.

'Archæology from the Sea: the Mahdia Wreck' translated from *Les Fouilles Sous-Marines de Mahdia*, by A. Merlin. La Revue Tunisienne, Institut de Carthage.

'A Royal Tomb at Ur' from *Excavations at Ur*, by Sir Leonard Woolley. Ernest Benn.

'The Winged Lions of Nimrud' from *Discoveries in the Ruins of Nineveh and Babylon*, by Sir Austen Layard. John Murray.

'Behistun: a Key to History' from *Notes on Some Paper Casts of Cuneiform Inscriptions upon the Sculptured Rock at Behistun exhibited to the Society of Antiquaries*, by Sir Henry Rawlinson, C.B., F.R.S., D.C.L. Published in *Archæologia* (Vol. XXXIV, 1852). Society of Antiquaries of London.

'Lascaux: a Painted Cave' from *Lascaux and Carnac*, by Glyn Daniel. Lutterworth Press.

'The Frozen Mammoth' from *The Mammoth*, by Bassett Digby. Witherby.

'The Mystery of Tollund Man' from an article published in the *Illustrated London News* of 24th November 1951, by Professor P. V. Glob of Aarhus University, Denmark.

'The Boy from the Lead Mountain' translated by Ann Orbach from 'El Nino del Cerro "El Plomo" ', by Grete Mostny. Article in the *Anais do XXXI Congresso Internacional de Americanistas* (Vol. II), São Paulo.

'Pompeii: a City Buried Alive' from *Pompeii: Its Life and Art*, by August Mau. The Macmillan Company, N.Y. Also from the translation of Pliny's *Letters* (Vol. I, Books vi, xvi and xx). Loeb Classical Library. Heinemann.